Responding to the Educational Needs of Today's Workplace

Ivan Charner, *Editor*
National Institute for Work and Learning

Catherine A. Rolzinski, *Editor*
Consultant

NEW DIRECTIONS FOR CONTINUING EDUCATION
GORDON G. DARKENWALD, *Editor-in-Chief*
Rutgers University

ALAN B. KNOX, *Consulting Editor*
University of Wisconsin

Number 33, Spring 1987

Paperback sourcebooks in
The Jossey-Bass Higher Education Series

Jossey-Bass Inc., Publishers
San Francisco • London

Ivan Charner, Catherine A. Rolzinski (eds.).
Responding to the Educational Needs of Today's Workplace.
New Directions for Continuing Education, no. 33.
San Francisco: Jossey-Bass, 1987.

New Directions for Continuing Education
Gordon G. Darkenwald, *Editor-in-Chief*
Alan B. Knox, *Consulting Editor*

Copyright © 1987 by Jossey-Bass Inc., Publishers
and
Jossey-Bass Limited

Copyright under International, Pan American, and Universal Copyright Conventions. All rights reserved. No part of this issue may be reproduced in any form—except for brief quotation (not to exceed 500 words) in a review or professional work—without permission in writing from the publishers.

New Directions for Continuing Education is published quarterly by Jossey-Bass Inc., Publishers (publication number USPS 493-930). Second-class postage paid at San Francisco, California, and at additional mailing offices. POSTMASTER: Send address changes to Jossey-Bass Inc., Publishers, 433 California Street, San Francisco, California 94104.

Editorial correspondence should be sent to the Editor-in-Chief, Gordon G. Darkenwald, Graduate School of Education, Rutgers University, 10 Seminary Place, New Brunswick, New Jersey 08903.

Library of Congress Catalog Card Number LC 85-644750

International Standard Serial Number ISSN 0195-2242

International Standard Book Number ISBN 1-55542-960-2

Cover art by WILLI BAUM

Manufactured in the United States of America

Ordering Information

The paperback sourcebooks listed below are published quarterly and can be ordered either by subscription or single copy.

Subscriptions cost $48.00 per year for institutions, agencies, and libraries. Individuals can subscribe at the special rate of $36.00 per year *if payment is by personal check*. (Note that the full rate of $48.00 applies if payment is by institutional check, even if the subscription is designated for an individual.) Standing orders are accepted.

Single copies are available at $11.95 when payment accompanies order. (California, New Jersey, New York, and Washington, D.C., residents please include appropriate sales tax.) For billed orders, cost per copy is $11.95 plus postage and handling.

Substantial discounts are offered to organizations and individuals wishing to purchase bulk quantities of Jossey-Bass sourcebooks. Please inquire.

Please note that these prices are for the academic year 1986-1987 and are subject to change without notice. Also, some titles may be out of print and therefore not available for sale.

To ensure correct and prompt delivery, all orders must give either the *name of an individual* or an *official purchase order number*. Please submit your order as follows:

Subscriptions: specify series and year subscription is to begin.
Single Copies: specify sourcebook code (such as, CE1) and first two words of title.

Mail orders for United States and Possessions, Australia, New Zealand, Canada, Latin America, and Japan to:
Jossey-Bass Inc., Publishers
433 California Street
San Francisco, California 94104

Mail orders for all other parts of the world to:
Jossey-Bass Limited
28 Banner Street
London EC1Y 8QE

New Directions for Continuing Education Series
Gordon G. Darkenwald, *Editor-in-Chief*
Alan D. Knox, *Consulting Editor*

CE1 *Enhancing Proficiencies of Continuing Educators,* Alan B. Knox
CE2 *Programming for Adults Facing Mid-Life Change,* Alan B. Knox
CE3 *Assessing the Impact of Continuing Education,* Alan B. Knox

CE4   *Attracting Able Instructors of Adults,* M. Alan Brown,
      Harlan G. Copeland
CE5   *Providing Continuing Education by Media and Technology,*
      Martin N. Chamberlain
CE6   *Teaching Adults Effectively,* Alan B. Knox
CE7   *Assessing Educational Needs of Adults,* Floyd C. Pennington
CE8   *Reaching Hard-to-Reach Adults,* Gordon G. Darkenwald,
      Gordon A. Larson
CE9   *Strengthening Internal Support for Continuing Education,*
      James C. Votruba
CE10 *Advising and Counseling Adult Learners,* Frank R. DiSilvestro
CE11 *Continuing Education for Community Leadership,* Harold W. Stubblefield
CE12 *Attracting External Funds for Continuing Education,* John H. Buskey
CE13 *Leadership Strategies for Meeting New Challenges,* Alan B. Knox
CE14 *Programs for Older Adults,* Morris A. Okun
CE15 *Linking Philosophy and Practice,* Sharan B. Merriam
CE16 *Creative Financing and Budgeting,* Travis Shipp
CE17 *Materials for Teaching Adults: Selection, Development, and Use,*
      John P. Wilson
CE18 *Strengthening Connections Between Education and Performance,*
      Stanley M. Grabowski
CE19 *Helping Adults Learn How to Learn,* Robert M. Smith
CE20 *Educational Outreach to Select Adult Populations,* Carol E. Kasworm
CE21 *Meeting Educational Needs of Young Adults,* Gordon G. Darkenwald,
      Alan B. Knox
CE22 *Designing and Implementing Effective Workshops,* Thomas J. Sork
CE23 *Realizing the Potential of Interorganizational Cooperation,* Hal Beder
CE24 *Evaluation for Program Improvement,* David Deshler
CE25 *Self-Directed Learning: From Theory to Practice,* Stephen Brookfield
CE26 *Involving Adults in the Educational Process,* Sandra H. Rosenblum
CE27 *Problems and Prospects in Continuing Professional Education,*
      Ronald M. Cervero, Craig L. Scanlan
CE28 *Improving Conference Design and Outcomes,* Paul J. Ilsley
CE29 *Personal Computers and the Adult Learner,* Barry Heermann
CE30 *Experiential and Simulation Techniques for Teaching Adults,*
      Linda H. Lewis
CE31 *Marketing Continuing Education,* Hal Beder
CE32 *Issues in Adult Career Counseling,* Juliet V. Miller, Mary Lynne Musgrove

Contents

Editors' Notes 1
Ivan Charner, Catherine A. Rolzinski

1. New Directions for Responding to a Changing Economy: 5
Integrating Education and Work
Ivan Charner, Catherine A. Rolzinski
Demographic, labor market, and technological changes are facing the economy. These changes call for new strategies and directions in continuing education that integrate education and work.

2. English-Language Training for the Workplace 17
Elizabeth F. Skinner, Nancy A. Siefer, Barbara A. Shovers
Effective English-language workplace programs require partnerships between education and industry based on reciprocal benefits, complementary skills and knowledge, and effective working relationships.

3. Developing a Computer-Integrated Manufacturing 27
Education Center
Victor Langer
Complex technical automation processes require "supertechs" to install, program, and maintain systems. Education and training that simulate the operating environments of industry can help serve the needs of both students and business.

4. The Business Development and Training Center: 39
An Educational Maintenance Organization
Lois Lamdin, Maxine Ballen Hassan
Built on the philosophy of the health maintenance organization, the educational maintenance organization creates an overall system of educational service and accountability. Developing a new approach to integrating education and work in a large corporate park requires planning, patience, and perseverance.

5. Worker Education for a Changing Economy: 49
New Labor-Academic Partnerships
Charles Derber
"Economic literacy" programs can provide workers with the tools necessary to chart their own economic future and to help them analyze, revitalize, and retool their own industries to combat the problems of industrial relocation and upheaval that are associated with foreign competition and new technology.

6. **Computer Education Opportunities for Rural Adults** 59
Mary Emery
Integrating education and work to provide computer literacy to rural adults helps foster local expertise in computer education and develop local leadership. The computer literacy curriculum and its delivery through a community-based system must recognize the values and life-styles of rural adults and communities.

7. **Educating Small Business for an International Marketplace** 67
Barbara H. Moebius
The importance of international trade requires new business skills and strategies. The International Trade Technical Center integrates education and work related to foreign trade for businesses and their employees.

8. **Improving Practice: Lessons from the Case Studies** 75
Catherine A. Rolzinski, Ivan Charner
What are the considerations for effectively integrating education and work? Changes in the economy require new directions for continuing education based on productive partnerships, learner-centered curricula, comprehensive services to individuals and organizations, and learning that empowers individuals and organizations not only to respond to but also to anticipate the changes they will be facing in the future.

9. **Critical Questions and Issues for Integrating Education and Work** 87
Ivan Charner, Catherine A. Rolzinski
How can continuing education better anticipate economic and technological changes in order to be proactive in its responses? What are the appropriate roles for businesses, unions, communities, government, and education in integrating education and work? These and other critical questions and issues suggest ways of looking at the future of integrating education and work.

Appendix. List of Projects of the FIPSE Education and the Economy Alliance 93

Index 97

Editors' Notes

Integrating education and work for adult workers has a long history and is, today, a growing enterprise. The first corporate school was set up in 1872 to train employees to meet the needs of industry. A little over 100 years later, corporate expenditures on education and training, to meet the needs of both industry and workers, have risen to over $40 billion annually ($210 billion if informal training is included). This sourcebook focuses on the expanding role of continuing and other forms of postsecondary education in relation to institutions of work (broadly conceived) and adult workers. It is particularly concerned with educational responses to changes in the economy—changes resulting from labor-force and demographic shifts, technological advances, and new business strategies and goals. Employers and employees are recognizing the need for continuing education and training in a rapidly changing world.

This volume is based on the assumption that the integration of education and work, whether formal or informal, is critical to the survival of our nation's economy. And, because of demographic shifts and the aging of the population, such integration is imperative to the survival of the education enterprise. The general purpose of this volume, then, is to examine how educational institutions can be responsive to the changing needs of industry and adult workers and to suggest how continuing education can develop and enhance programs that integrate education and work.

This sourcebook is a direct outgrowth of a project supported by the Fund for the Improvement of Postsecondary Education (FIPSE) of the U.S. Department of Education. The FIPSE Education and the Economy Alliance is a group of twenty-five projects concerned with improving postsecondary education's ability to respond to changes in the economy. A list of the projects is provided in the Appendix at the end of this sourcebook. Each project offers a unique lesson in integrating education and work. Six of the projects are highlighted in this sourcebook through short case studies. They were selected, not because they were better or more innovative, but rather because they represent diverse approaches to the issues central to integrating education and work effectively.

As the reader will see, there are a number of common themes that run across these (and the other nineteen) projects. First, these projects are responding to a problem or to a set of problems that directly result from changing economic realities. Second, the population being served by these projects is adults, most of whom are or have been in the work force and can best be served by continuing education. Finally, each of the projects is built on some form of partnership or collaboration between education

1

and other organizations which include businesses, organized labor, and community groups.

The first chapter, by Charner and Rolzinski, establishes the context for the sourcebook. It provides an overview of the economic, demographic, and technological changes facing the economy for the remainder of this century and well into the next. We then present a framework for exploring new ways to integrate education and work in response to these changes.

Chapters Two through Seven present case studies of six endeavors that integrate education and work for groups as diverse as limited-English-proficient workers, rural adults, unions, small businesses, and a corporate park. In Chapter Two, Skinner, Siefer, and Shovers present evidence that only when education and industry truly work together can effective English-language (and other) workplace programs result. Through their case study of an innovative English-language training program, the authors lay out three essential prerequisites to productive partnerships that integrate education and work: reciprocal benefits; complementary skills and knowledge; and effective working relationships.

Langer, in Chapter Three, portrays the development of a computer-integrated manufacturing education center to meet the needs of local industry for "supertechs" who can install, program, and maintain high-technology manufacturing and engineering equipment and systems. The program is designed around computer-based labs that simulate the operating environments of local industries. Through extensive partnerships with businesses, which donate equipment, provide assistance in curriculum design, and offer training workshops, the program integrates education and work not only for recent high school graduates but also for full-time employees in need of retraining.

Chapter Four, by Lamdin and Hassan, examines the development and operation of an "educational maintenance organization" in a large corporate park. The case study of the Business Development and Training Center provides answers to these questions: What are the critical elements of the educational maintenance idea, and how does it become a reality?

Derber's Chapter Five describes a partnership formed between an educational institution and local labor unions in order to help combat the problems of industrial dislocation and upheaval associated with foreign competition and new technology. The resulting "economic literacy" project provides a social, historical, and economic education to workers, giving them the tools to chart their own economic future and to help them analyze, revitalize, and retool their own industries.

As Emery makes clear in Chapter Six, integrating education and work to provide computer education opportunities to rural adults can affect both individuals and communities. The case study examines the development of a computer literacy curriculum and its community-based delivery system. By providing computer, curricular, and human resources to local communities, the project helps to foster local expertise in computer education and in leadership development.

In Chapter Seven, Moebius argues that the increased importance of international markets to local economies requires the development of new business skills and strategies. Small and medium-sized businesses need to be trained in international trade if they are going to compete in the global marketplace. This case study describes the continuing education programs offered by the International Trade Technical Center. The center integrates education and work related to foreign trade for businesses and their employees in order to increase their awareness of the global economy, to facilitate exporting, and to develop new employment opportunities.

Rolzinski and Charner explore the lessons learned from the case studies in Chapter Eight. We then present, in Chapter Nine, a set of critical questions and issues for the consideration of continuing education program developers, practitioners, and policy makers. These questions suggest ways to look at future possibilities for integrating education and work. If continuing education is to respond adequately to changes in the economy, then new policies and practices must be adopted that are responsive to the needs and demands of working adults, businesses, and communities.

It is our hope that this sourcebook will provide examples and insights into strategies for integrating education and work effectively. We hope that the case studies provide practical advice and assistance to continuing educators and others who serve or wish to serve adult workers, communities, and businesses. We also hope to challenge these same audiences to improve the ways in which they address changing demographic and economic realities by developing new partnerships that meet the specific needs of adult learners in their localities.

Ivan Charner
Catherine A. Rolzinski
Editors

Ivan Charner is director of research and development at the National Institute for Work and Learning in Washington, D.C. He was project director for the FIPSE-funded Education and the Economy Alliance project.

Catherine A. Rolzinski is a consultant in the areas of education and economic development based in Washington, D.C. She has also served as the program officer at the Department of Education's Fund for the Improvement of Postsecondary Education with lead responsibility over the Education and the Economy Alliance.

Both the clients and the mission of adult and continuing education are changing and will continue to change as a result of demographic, economic, and technological shifts in the economy.

New Directions for Responding to a Changing Economy: Integrating Education and Work

Ivan Charner, Catherine A. Rolzinski

Continuing and postsecondary education strategies for the future will depend on the characteristics of tomorrow's learners as well as the nature of the changing economy. We can be fairly certain about the demographic composition and educational needs of the traditional college-age population of eighteen- to twenty-four-year-olds. We are less certain, however, about the makeup of adult learners of the future and about the effect that changes in the economy will have on educational policies, programs, and practices. One thing that seems certain is that we will need a better integration of education and work if our nation's productivity and economic viability are to improve and if the postsecondary education enterprise is to survive at its current levels. Whether in terms of formal partnerships between educational institutions and businesses or in terms of the preparation and retraining of human resources, education and work need to be more closely integrated. Nowhere is this more critical than in continuing education, whose mandate is to serve the needs of adult learners and, to an ever-increasing extent, the needs of business and industry.

I. Charner, C. A. Rolzinski (eds.). *Responding to the Educational Needs of Today's Workplace.*
New Directions for Continuing Education, no. 33. San Francisco: Jossey-Bass, Spring 1987.

We begin by tracing the structural changes facing the economy throughout the remainder of this century and well into the next. We then introduce a framework for examining the resources that comprise the adult and continuing education system, and we use this framework to explore new strategies for integrating education and work.

Structural Changes Through the Twentieth Century

Continuing education policies and practices are developed in response to a complex set of factors. As we move toward the twenty-first century, a number of these factors are changing: the population, for example, is aging; the information industry is becoming a dominant force in the economy; and technological advances are rapidly changing the employment picture.

Continuing educators can choose between two types of response to these changes. In the first, continuing education takes a reactive posture; new strategies are developed in direct response to changes that have already taken place. The second type of response is a more proactive one, in which continuing educators try to predict the changes—through research, analysis, and some luck—and develop new strategies in anticipation of the changes. Such an approach involves greater risks, but the payoffs in terms of preparing individuals and institutions for economic change should offset the risks. Because it is not always possible to predict change, continuing education by necessity will have to employ both types of responses simultaneously.

In this section, we present the major social and demographic, economic, and technological shifts predicted for the next quarter century, focusing on their consequences for the workplace and other institutions. New strategies and considerations for continuing education and for integrating education and work are presented later in the chapter.

Social and Demographic Shifts. The changes in the composition of the U.S. population and in the composition of its labor force have both direct and indirect consequences for adult and continuing education.

Aging of the Population. Since the baby boom of the 1940s and the 1950s, the U.S. population has been aging. The number of young adults (sixteen to twenty-four years old) will decline between 1980 and 1995, affecting the pool of traditional-age college entrants and the pool of entry-level workers in the labor force.

The 1980s and 1990s will see the baby-boom generation move into middle age, increasing the number of workers thirty to forty-nine years old by 79 percent. By the year 2000, the median age of the U.S. citizenry will be almost thirty-five. The labor market behaviors and attitudes of this cohort of workers will be affected by "generational crowding" or "midcareer compaction." That is, there will be far fewer of the job and career promotions usually associated with the midcareer stage than there will be middle-aged workers. One consequence of this phenomenon is that many in this cohort will need to make major career and life shifts, looking to other work and nonwork opportunities for their financial, social, and personal rewards.

Medical and nutritutional advances will continue to increase life expectancies. While many older workers will retire early, others will remain in or re-enter the labor force, for financial, social, and psychological reasons. New work patterns are expected that will enable these older workers to work part-time (daily, weekly, monthly, or yearly) while pursuing other activities traditionally associated with retirement. Services and resources for these older persons will be needed on a scale that will only be surpassed when the baby-boom generation moves into its older years in 2025.

More Women and Minorities in the Labor Force. The numbers and proportion of women in the paid labor force have been steadily growing. It is estimated that women will comprise 65 percent of all new hires during the next ten years and over half of the labor force before the end of the century. At the same time, the population of blacks and Hispanics in the U.S. work force will steadily increase. By the year 2000, these two groups will constitute almost one-quarter of the work force. Increased immigration (legal and illegal) is expected as a result of shortages of entry-level workers. The impact of the increased proportion of minorities also will be felt by schools, government, and service organizations.

Economic Shifts. Major economic shifts and corresponding changes in the employment sector have occurred over the past two decades, and further shifts are expected through the first quarter of the next century. Some of these shifts have been or will be dramatic, while others will be more gradual. What we produce, how we produce, the way we work, and the distribution of jobs are changing and will continue to change. While the speed of these changes has clear implications for continuing education policies and practices, it is the changes themselves that will have the major impact on the future of continuing education.

Decline of the Industrial Sector. In 1984, 30 percent of the work force was employed in the industrial sector. However, this sector has been declining since the early 1950s, and the decline is expected to continue through the next decade, due, in large part, to increased automation and robotization, improved operational procedures, and competition from developing countries with low labor costs. This sector is expected to employ only 11 to 12 percent of the work force by the mid 1990s. The automobile, steel, clothing, and support industries have been affected by the growing trend of importing, which has led to large numbers of displaced or dislocated industrial workers.

Growth of the Service Sector. The service sector is, by far, the dominant sector of employment with about two-thirds of the work force employed in service jobs in 1984. Over 80 percent of the employment growth projected through 1995 is expected to occur in the service sector. The growth of this sector is due to a number of factors: First, the growing proportion of women in the paid work force is increasing the number of dual-income households (75 percent by 1995). These households are "short" on time but "long" on money, and consequently they "buy" more time by purchasing more services, such as meals, home repair, dependent care, and education. In addition, there is an increase in the number of single-parent households, which may not be "long" on money but will need to purchase many services, nonetheless.

A second factor that will affect the growth of this sector will be the millions of workers displaced by automation, technological advances, and foreign competition. Since many service jobs involve relatively unsophisticated, commonplace skills and knowledge, the service sector has always been the natural employer of last resort. The ready supply of displaced workers with limited employable skills will lead to low wages in parts of the service sector and thus will promote the general growth of service-related business. Millions of people use low-level service employment as a transitional phase in their careers, while they acquire some form of retraining to qualify for work in higher-paying jobs in the service and other sectors of the economy.

Continued Growth in Self-Employment. Self-employment, which reached a low of 7 percent in 1970, has been on the rise since then and is expected to continue to grow. The growth of the service sector and of the information industry within all of the sectors, will reinforce this rise by encouraging independent information and service entrepreneurs. It is projected that self-employment will double by the year 2000 from its low point of 1970. As midlevel, midcareer workers are laid off or not promoted, they will be "forced" to become self-employed in new venture enterprises. Others will see the opportunities for self-realization, independence, and personal advancement in starting their own businesses. The computer software and support industries provide clear examples of this growing phenomenon.

Growth of International Trade and Third-World Development. Developed countries are rapidly using up their reserves of natural resources while continuing to upgrade the quality of human resources. This will cause increased dependence on developing nations for raw materials and "cheap" labor for mass-produced goods. It is projected that, by the year 2000, one-third of the world's goods and services will be consumed or used outside of the country of origin.

Technological Shifts. From microcomputers to robots, word processors, and genetic engineering, we have witnessed rapid advances in technology in the past two to three decades. These new applied technologies have affected every sector in the labor force and in the general society.

Agricultural advances have allowed fewer and fewer farmers to produce more and more. The microcomputer and word processor have transformed the office from one that is largely labor intensive to one that relies heavily on electronic storage and transmission of information, creating the "paperless office." Automation has transformed the assembly lines and factory floors in many industries by using robots to perform the tasks of large numbers of workers. Computer-aided design (CAD) and computer-aided manufacturing (CAM) have been used in a wide array of industries to design and produce new products and systems. Communication has also been affected by new technologies. Teleconferencing (video and audio), satellite systems, videotext, and car phones are just a few of the new communications technologies that have emerged in the past few years. The advances in biological and health sciences, as a result of technological change, are no less staggering.

The high-technology revolution is all around us—in the factory, at the office, in our communication, transportation, and health care systems, and in our homes. The growth of these technologies will continue, but the implications for employment, social relations, and personal development are yet to be recognized fully.

Creation and Elimination of Jobs. Robotization, CAD/CAM systems, and other new manufacturing and industrial technologies are projected to eliminate 5 to 7 million jobs (mostly blue collar) before the turn of the century. Information and communication technologies, on the other hand, are expected to eliminate 7 to 12 million white-collar positions. The total loss of jobs is projected to be between 15 and 20 million by the year 2000. At the same time, the production of these new technologies will create 2 to 3 million new jobs, while positions related to the maintenance and repair of these new technologies will generate an additional 4 to 5 million high-technology service positions. In addition, these new technologies will affect the production of finished information products (books, magazines, disks, cassettes, and video media) in their "publishing" industry. Between 1.5 and 2.5 million jobs are expected to be generated in this area. The net result is a loss of between 5 and 13 million jobs due to the new technologies.

Collaborative Approaches to Human Resources Management. While new applied technologies will affect the workplace, productivity will also be affected by the "social technologies" used to organize and coordinate human resources. Recent workplace research, which has been brought into sharp focus by comparisons with foreign competitors, suggests that more collaborative, decentralized workplace arrangements and human resource management technologies (such as quality circles, job enrichment, joint union/labor agreements, and so on) possess a far greater potential for increasing productive capacity than do purely technological innovations.

Collaborative approaches to human resources management are

being pursued successfully at all levels of operation in private and public, large and small organizations. The potential impact of such collaborative approaches, however, is dependent on their acceptance by all levels of employees and by the wider society.

The structural changes that are anticipated for the next twenty-five years are sure to affect the work force, the workplace, the lives of workers, and society in general. The combined effects of the ongoing economic transition, the changing demography of the population and the work force, and the nation's assimilation of new applied technologies assure a steadily increasing demand for training, education, and human resource development. The critical question is not what the overall level of investment in education, training, and human service development should be, but rather, *how* continuing educators and trainers should respond to these changes.

Strategies for Integrating Education and Work

In this section, we will develop a framework for analyzing continuing education resources and for exploring new strategies and directions for integrating education and work.

The framework has four major elements, which are related to each other in a dynamic way. The four elements are clients, content, modes of delivery, and sources; these are the resources that comprise the continuing education system. The framework recognizes that the relations among the elements are affected by two sets of external factors: the changing economy, and the policies regulating education and training processes and economic behavior.

Clients. At the center of the continuing education system are the clients. Clients are the students and organizations who use education and training services. While adults are the most obvious client group, businesses, community groups, unions, and the government must also be considered clients of the system.

As the needs of different client groups change, so must continuing education offerings. For example, the changing demographics suggest new strategies related to preretirement education, retirement programs, basic adult literacy, and English-language programs, to name a few. The economic changes suggest, among others, programs in small-business development and international trade, while the technological changes will require retraining programs as well as programs on collaborative approaches to human resource management.

Whether preparing individuals to meet the challenges of a new job, a new career, or a new phase of life or helping businesses and other organizations respond to changing economic and technological factors, continuing education clearly must be based on strategies that integrate education and work. By working with representatives of business, government, labor, and community organization on planning committees or teams, continuing educators can identify their future clients and take the lead in developing proactive education and training programs for them.

Content. The content of continuing education consists of the skills, knowledge, and attitudes directly and indirectly transmitted to clients. It also includes support services for individuals and organizations. Seven broad content categories include:
- General/liberal education
- Basic skills
- Vocational skills
- Skill retraining
- Skill upgrading
- Management and professional training
- Support services, such as:
    a. Counseling
    b. Information
    c. Basic and applied research
    d. Economic and community development.

Changes in economic, demographic, and technological conditions have affected and will continue to affect the content of continuing education programs. For some programs, these changes mean being more responsive to the needs of local businesses, while, for others, they result in new programs that focus on the individual adult learner and offer courses in basic skills and literacy, retraining, or skill upgrading.

The changing education needs of the workplace and the economy suggest a content for continuing education that is characterized by diversity. Continuing education must work with businesses and adult learners to anticipate the diverse needs of these diverse clients. A second strategy for identifying the content needs of the future is through the analysis of the economic development and human resource needs of a community. For example, if a community has a large population of factory workers approaching retirement, a concerted preretirement education program would be called for. If this same community is facing plant closings, programs that prepare people for new jobs in the service and information sectors or in new technologies would be needed. The point is to develop content for continuing education that not only responds to the immediate needs of its clients but also anticipates their future needs.

Modes of Delivery. Modes of delivery are the ways in which content is made available to clients. Modes of delivery comprise the methods, timing, and location of instruction as well as the means by which support services are delivered.

Methods of instruction can be formal, experiential, or informal. Formal instruction most often follows an explicit set of content guidelines and employs lecture, discussion, exercises, or experiments, and other classroom-based activities. The majority of continuing education instruction utilizes such formal approaches.

The experiential or experience-based method of instruction is growing in popularity, particularly among teachers of older learners and of adults engaged in skill training. In experiential learning, the learner engages in an activity or activities that are closely related to the desired instructional outcomes. Teaching follows a more implicit set of content guidelines. This type of instruction tends to be more practical, but it also often has a theoretical component. Using entrepreneurial skills as an example will help clarify the distinction between the formal and experiential methods of instruction.

The delivery of entrepreneurial skills can be accomplished through the use of textbooks, lectures, and discussions. In this case, an explicit curriculum is followed to teach the elements of successful small-business operation. An experiential approach would have learners participate in a small business (through an "incubator" program or a simulation, for example, or by apprenticing under a small-business mentor). In this situation, elements of small-business operation are learned through the actual experience of running a business; the content is transmitted implicitly. It should be noted that these two methods are not mutually exclusive, and many instructors combine the two.

By "informal methods of instruction," we mean opportunities outside of an educational program, through which individuals can acquire norms, values, information, knowledge, expectations, skills, and can learn roles. These opportunities most often occur because of membership in a group or because of interaction with an individual. Here, content is neither implicitly nor explicitly transmitted. Rather, through generalized others (Mead, 1934), reference groups (Hyman and Singer, 1968), role models (Merton, 1965), significant others (Sullivan, 1947), or symbolic models (Bandura, 1971), informal instruction and learning take place.

Timing and location of instruction are the other two components of modes of delivery. Timing relates to the "when" and "how long," while location relates to the "where" of instruction. Continuing education has been a pioneer in varying the patterns of timing and location to respond to the needs of different clients. To provide the integration of education and work for diverse clients of the future, educators will need to continue to offer instruction in workplaces, communities, union halls, over the radio and television, through computers, and in other nontraditional locations. In addition, planners will have to continue to offer programs of varying lengths (such as one-day seminars and workshops, weekend programs, and multisession courses) at varying times—namely, during the summer, weekends, early morning, evening, and so on.

In summary, it is essential for all strategies for integrating education and work to vary their modes of delivery to respond to the needs of different clients. This means increasing the programs' reliance on experiential and informal methods of instruction and on the use of computers, radio, television, audio and video cassettes, and other new technologies. It also calls for continued diversity in terms of when, how long, and where programs are offered.

Sources. Sources are the institutions that transmit skills, knowledge, and attitudes to individuals. While the home (family), the community, and mass media are all sources of instruction, for the purposes of this framework we focus on education and training institutions and the workplace. We will identify here three specific types of such sources.

The first of these sources are the public and private institutions of higher education, including universities, two- and four-year colleges, and vocational and technical schools. These schools transmit information, knowledge, skills, and attitudes directly through the content of their programs and course offerings and indirectly through interactions with individuals and groups within the schools. To an increasing extent, especially with the growth of two-year colleges and continuing education, these institutions are serving diverse target populations, including adult workers, businesses, unions, and community groups.

The second source is the workplace, which is offering strong competition to the traditional institutions of higher education through a "shadow education" system. This system comprises corporate training offices and institutes. Corporate training offices offer formal and informal education and training programs to employees; these programs usually involve skill training or retraining, skill upgrading, management and professional training, and basic skills instruction. Training institutes also have been set up by large corporations to respond to specific needs for their work force. These institutes can operate within an organization or external to it as separate entities set up by the corporation.

The third source of continuing education and training are private skills training institutions and individuals. Associations, unions, consulting firms, service organizations, proprietary schools, and individual consultants can offer programs and services. Today, associations such as the American Banking Institute, the American Management Association, and private training organizations offer more programs and have more students than all traditional postsecondary education institutions combined. Service organizations, such as community service agencies and churches, offer a wide array of continuing education, training, and services. Through funds provided in collective bargaining agreements, cooperation with colleges and universities, and their own financial support, unions have created a variety of mechanisms to support the higher education of workers through financial subsidies and program delivery. Private proprietary schools offer training in specific skill areas such as secretarial science, beauty sciences, dental technology, drafting, computer programming, and business. Finally, the increase in the number of private consultants who offer training and other services to corporations, social groups, and individuals has been nothing short of phenomenal. From self-help to speed reading, from career or life planning to specific skills training, private consultants provide a wide range of continuing education and training programs.

The magnitude and diversity of these often competing sources of continuing education require new ways of combining education and work for the very survival of the traditional continuing education enterprise. Through partnerships with businesses, organized labor, government, and community groups, continuing education can carve out its territory for delivery of educational and training programs and services. Some overlap of programs among the different sources of continuing education is both necessary and inevitable; too much overlap, however, will benefit neither the sources nor the clients of continuing education programs.

Summary

The conceptual framework that has been developed presents a means of examining the resources that comprise the continuing education system and of exploring new strategies for integrating education and work. These new strategies must accommodate a number of common themes: First, the clients of continuing education are not only adult learners but also businesses, unions, community organizations, and government agencies. The needs and wants of all of these clients must be assessed in relation to the changes in demographic, economic, and technological conditions.

Second, new content and modes of delivery need to be developed that will be responsive to these diverse clients. Content must be learner or client driven; relevant to the life situations of the learners or to the nature and characteristics of the businesses, unions, or community groups; and responsive to local and national economic and demographic realities.

Third, methods, timing, and location of instruction have undergone dramatic changes. Methods that continue to experiment with experiential, self-directed, technology-assisted, and peer-led strategies will be needed. Also, new timing schemes that have no boundaries on when, how long, or where a program will be are essential.

Fourth, because the sources of continuing education include corporations, associations, other organizations, and individuals, traditional providers of continuing education will need to be more "businesslike" in their approach to marketing and more responsive to the needs of clients. By working with these other providers, problems of overlap and "turfdom" can be reduced.

Changes in continuing education resources will result in new directions for programs, and the development of partnerships with other institutions and organizations offers an effective approach to dealing with these changes. Through partnerships with businesses, unions, community groups, and government agencies, continuing educators will be able to offer educational programs and services that both respond to and anticipate changes occurring in society.

References

Bandura, A. "Analysis of Modeling Processes." In A. Bandura (ed.), *Psychological Modeling: Conflicting Theories.* New York: Lieber-Atherton, 1971.
Hyman, H., and Singer, E. *Readings in Reference Group Theory and Research.* New York: Free Press, 1968.
Mead, G. *Mind, Self, and Society.* Chicago: University of Chicago Press, 1934.
Merton, R. *Social Theory and Social Structure.* New York: Free Press, 1965.
Sullivan, H. *Conception of Modern Psychiatry.* Washington, D.C.: White Psychiatric Foundation, 1947.

Ivan Charner is director of research and development at the National Institute for Work and Learning in Washington, D.C.

Catherine A. Rolzinski is a consultant in the areas of education and economic development based in Washington, D.C.

An English-language program in the workplace is implemented, achieving the objectives of the employer, liberal education, and limited-English-proficient workers.

English-Language Training for the Workplace

Elizabeth F. Skinner, Nancy A. Siefer, Barbara A. Shovers

The workplace provides a rich source of information about language use in our society today. The accelerated pace of change, the increasing dependence on technology, and new styles of participatory management produce a work environment that is highly interactive. Success in all job positions, even at the entry level, now requires high levels of communication skills. New forms of language use are emerging to fit the demands of this language-oriented workplace.

An understanding of the dynamics of language in relation to work is valuable to educators because language competence remains one of the essential characteristics of the educated person in our culture. It is equally important to industry because it clarifies the nature of job proficiency in today's language-rich work settings. Future approaches to education and training, to be effective, must be based on such a practical understanding of communicative proficiency. This understanding requires the combined perspectives of education and industry.

Recently, Arizona State University (ASU) and Honeywell, Inc., collaborated on a project, Language Working, which investigated the nature of language use within one facility of Honeywell's Large Computer Prod-

I. Charner, C. A. Rolzinski (eds.). *Responding to the Educational Needs of Today's Workplace.*
New Directions for Continuing Education, no. 33. San Francisco: Jossey-Bass, Spring 1987.

ucts Division. The information gained through this study was used to design an English-language training program for Honeywell employees who were limited in their ability to communicate on the job because their native language was not English.

In this chapter, we explore the way in which this project was able to generate insights about language and work that are vital both to liberal education and to education for work. Following a brief description of the project, we explore how natural and productive a partnership between education and industry can be when three essential prerequisites are met:

1. *Reciprocal benefits.* Both partners must anticipate and receive concrete benefit from the partnership. In addition, each must be cognizant of the benefits anticipated by the other and facilitate their attainment.

2. *Complementary skills and knowledge.* The partners must recognize their need for each other. Each must bring skills and knowledge not possessed by the other that are critical to the project's success.

3. *Effective working relationship.* The partners must establish a structure within which they can interact effectively. The structure must be flexible and dynamic in nature.

Project Profile

The Language Working project was designed to improve the employment situation of workers from linguistic minorities by helping these workers increase their ability to use English to communicate in the workplace. To achieve this goal, the project team carried out a needs assessment, designed a curriculum, and piloted a training program.

Needs Assessment. The first objective of the Language Working project was to observe and document the language skills needed by limited-English-proficient workers to function effectively in their job positions.

Fieldwork at the site lasted six months. The project staff interviewed managers, trainers, and first-line supervisors or "group leaders." Once accepted by these supervisory personnel, the staff visited the individual work areas and talked with limited-English-proficient (LEP) workers and their native English-speaking coworkers. Multiple perspectives were gained about the language skills needed to be an effective worker. At the same time, support for the project was growing at all levels.

The staff asked to see copies of the instruction manuals available for each type of job in manufacturing. In addition, any other written documents or forms required to carry out job procedures were collected. These materials revealed much about the nature of the job tasks as well as the literacy demands that the workers face each day. Our observations helped us to detail the types of interactions that occur among workers and to identify the nature of the communication skills involved in those interactions.

Without exception, English-language instructors who operate programs in the workplace complained of inadequate preparation and insufficient understanding of the workplace environment. We wanted to develop a process through which future programs could prepare instructors efficiently and effectively. Throughout the needs-assessment phase of the project, the staff paid attention to process as well as content.

Curriculum Development. The second objective of the project was to utilize the information gained through the needs assessment to develop materials for a language training program. The curriculum that resulted consisted of five modules, each one dealing with a type of workplace event in which communication skills were especially important. The modules were entitled "Training," "Handling Routine Problems," "Breaks," "Meetings," and "Job Advancement."

The syllabi for these modules are organized functionally. In other words, each module is structured around a number of key functions or purposes for language use. Any specific language skills, such as grammar or pronunciation, are embedded within this functional structure. For example, the module on breaks, which deals with informal social language, is organized around such functions as sharing personal information, joking, and expressing feelings.

This type of functional format, developed in Europe in the 1970s, is becoming increasingly popular in this country for teaching foreign languages and English as a second language. It is especially appropriate for work-related instruction because it ensures that the training will always be relevant. Potentially meaningless drill work is embued with meaning when used to support a focus on authentic purposes for communication in familiar workplace events. It guarantees that what is practiced in the classroom will be practiced immediately and reinforced during the rest of the workday.

Pilot Training Program. The modules were piloted in an eighteen-week program taught on site at Honeywell during work hours. Thirty-six students were enrolled in one of three classes based on their level of English-language proficiency. Class sessions lasted one and a half hours, were held twice a week, and included a range of activities from skill practice, discussion, and role play to simulations. The staff communicated periodically with the managers and first-line supervisors of the students to inform them of what was being taught in the class and to seek their views on the students' progress. In addition, a cross-cultural training session was held for these supervisors to help them learn how to communicate better with their limited-English-speaking employees.

Reciprocal Benefits

Industry Perspective. Because of the changes Honeywell was undergoing at the time when the Language Working partnership was being formed, they were very open to participation. Like most companies in the computer-related industries, Honeywell's Large Computer Products Division (LCPD) was "downsizing" and reconfiguring its work force. As a result, the company was well aware that its reduced work force would need to be highly and flexibly skilled. The rapid pace of change in the industry would call on the remaining employees to be continually retrained and cross-trained. At the same time, the company was undergoing a "culture change" by adopting an approach to participatory management. All employees would be expected to participate in work and quality involvement teams to carry out production, solve problems, and provide creative input to company policies. Honeywell needed flexible workers able to learn quickly, think critically, and communicate effectively.

The company recognized that not all employees, though technically skilled, had the communication skills needed to meet the challenges of this new work environment. This was especially true of the limited-English-proficient workers who spoke English as their second language. At Honeywell's LCPD, these workers were primarily Hispanic and Southeast Asian in background; most had been working for the company for at least six years. Because these LEP workers were highly skilled and loyal employees, the company wanted to make an investment in developing their communicative competence.

The Arizona State University staff anticipated that the company would expect to see concrete benefits from the project in terms of more productive workers, fewer product defects, and, ultimately, dollars saved. Supervisors found that they could indeed document the outcome of the project in these terms. They were able to provide the company with such reports of positive changes in worker productivity as the following: "This program has saved the company a lot of money. Bad communication is costly. There have been fewer mistakes since the course began. The program is well worth it," and "I think the class does save money for the company because of better communication. We get better feedback, improved worker productivity, and quality of work. The class has benefited our area. Workers are happier and more productive."

Supervisors were able to estimate how much money the program had saved the company by considering the savings in employee time. Increased communication skills meant less time was spent explaining procedures and handling problems. One supervisor, for example, reported that, for each of the four LEP workers in his area, he saved approximately one hour per week of the worker's time and one hour of his own time. Taking their hourly salaries into account, this time saving translated into a dollar saving of $84 a week or $4,000 a year for this one area.

Educator's Perspective. From an educator's perspective, the value of the Language Working project came from its potential to generate a knowledge base, not previously available, for work-related language instruction.

The ASU staff saw this possibility as exciting both theoretically and practically. An important characteristic of the fieldwork was that it emphasized the functional aspects of language learning. This emphasis was influenced by two perspectives: the pragmatic, which views language in terms of what it accomplishes in the world, and the sociolinguistic, which insists that language be seen within its social and cultural context. From both of these theoretical viewpoints, studies of language as it functions in the concrete, outcome-oriented world of work are especially significant.

Practically, the functional emphasis was motivated by a desire to make language instruction more relevant to the needs of learners. Discontent with traditional academic forms of language instruction has been increasing worldwide. Students are demanding instruction that can prepare them to use language skills in real-life settings, and, for most students, the workplace is the most important domain for language use.

The ASU staff wanted to make a practical and theoretical contribution to the field through the Language Working project. The Honeywell participants, realizing this, took the time to provide the detailed information ASU needed. They provided the facilities and resources required to do in-depth and holistic assessments of language learning needs. They allowed researchers to interact with employees and provided access to work areas for detailed observations. In addition, the company worked with the staff in preparing materials, including videotapes for presentations to professional organizations.

In short, both Honeywell and ASU benefited from the Language Working program. Honeywell viewed the program as developing an important aspect of work proficiency that resulted in more productive workers, lower product defect rates, and increased profits. The ASU staff viewed the program as an opportunity to explore an important area of need in language teaching and to develop an innovative curriculum to meet that need. These perspectives, though different, proved to be compatible and mutually supportive.

Complementary Skills and Knowledge

The ASU staff required continual help from their Honeywell partners. This was true for a number of reasons. As educators, the ASU team experienced a kind of culture shock in entering the world of industry. They needed insiders to serve as informants in order to help them enter what was for them a strange setting, to avoid breaking the rules of acceptable conduct, and to learn their way around. The environment was difficult to negotiate both physically (because the buildings were labyrinthian) and socially (because the organizational structure was complex and dynamic).

Further, although the ASU partners knew much about curriculum organization and presentation, they could not make decisions on their own about the content of a language training program for Honeywell because they lacked knowledge about the nature of communication at Honeywell. They needed the expertise of "natives" in order to identify the purposes and situations for language use in that specific context.

Honeywell, while generally aware of the problems caused by lack of language proficiency on the part of some employees, did not have the knowledge or skills to define the problem and formulate an educational solution. They realized that their usual strategies for problem solving and that their standard approaches to skills training were not appropriate. On the other hand, previous attempts to rely totally on educators by sending LEP employees to general English-as-a-second-language courses had failed to produce improvements in communication skills on the job. The company realized that they needed to collaborate with educators if an effective instructional program was to be possible.

After six months of interaction between ASU researchers and Honeywell, a language training program was designed that was uniquely appropriate to the workplace in terms of both instructional approach and content. Five situations emerged as especially central to communication at Honeywell: training; handling routine problems on the job; social language at breaks; meetings; and job advancement. Within these situations, a variety of functions or purposes for language use were prominent, including, for example, establishing social contact, following instructions, indicating lack of understanding, seeking information, reporting problems, and understanding jokes.

These situations and purposes, which could not have been derived without the intensive interaction between educators and workers, provided the structure and fabric of an effective language training program. In addition, decisions about scheduling, student placement, and other aspects of the logistics of course delivery could be made based on a thorough understanding of the work context; this, in turn, allowed the program to be integrated effectively into the workers' week. Choices of instructional strategy and design of materials could be made with consideration for the characteristics of the workers and the forms of training and instruction that they were already experiencing.

Effective Working Relationship

Although the company's motivation to participate was high, the Language Working project could not have achieved its goals if an effective structure had not been established through which the ASU and Honeywell partners could interact. Despite enthusiasm about expected benefits and mutual respect, educators and employers are most likely to abandon partnerships of this type early on because of differences in customary approaches to work. The participants become frustrated, time and energy are wasted in unproductive effort, and misunderstandings become increasingly damaging.

To avoid such negative consequences, the structure of relationships between educators and the workplace must be flexible enough to survive the frequent changes that occur in the workplace. Such flexibility involves the ability to adjust quickly to changes in personnel. In a little more than two years, the Honeywell liaison person with ASU changed three times. In addition, many of the key members of the partnership changed their job positions and locations within the company several times when major staff reorganizations occurred. Each time such a "break" occurred in the partnership, quick action was required by both Honeywell and ASU to repair the damage and protect the working relationship.

Flexibility was also required in terms of the direction and scope of the project as information emerged about communication in the workplace that influenced decisions about who needed to be involved in the partnership. For example, as workers were identified with potential need for training in communication skills, new managers and supervisors had to become involved in the planning. As the importance of the job manuals became evident, the staff needed to interact with the planning engineers who produced them and the personnel responsible for revising them. On the other hand, some changes meant less involvement for some individuals who were originally quite centrally involved. As the company decreased its reliance on temporary workers, for instance, it became less important to involve those staff members responsible for temporary workers.

To maintain the necessary flexibility, the partnership must have a structure that is supported through multiple contacts. For the Language Working project, multiple contacts were established on both sides of the partnership. The first contact between ASU and Honeywell came through the Human Resources Division. The staff maintained this connection after a liaison person was assigned to them in the Training Division. The liaison made certain that several other trainers became well informed about the project. This meant that, even if the liaison was unavailable, problems could be handled immediately and opportunities would not be missed. On the other side, since the seven members of the ASU staff interacted very closely with each other on all aspects of the project, any member could represent the others in interaction with Honeywell if this became necessary. In most cases, Honeywell could get immediate attention from ASU when problems arose or communication was necessary.

In addition, meetings were held at Honeywell with middle managers and first-line supervisors so that information about the project was widely available. A number of these individuals showed special interest in what they heard and became key providers of information for the ASU staff throughout the project. Through these managers and supervisors, the project was able to extend its web of relationships horizontally to other supervisory staff and vertically to workers and to upper management.

Several months into the project, the ASU staff and its Honeywell liaison made a presentation to upper management and gained official endorsement. One member of the vice-president's staff was especially vocal in supporting the project. The ASU staff followed up on his expressed interest, and he became a key part of the partnership.

The complex net of connections between ASU and Honeywell provided continuing communication. The ASU staff could share frequent progress reports and receive reactions and suggestions from a cross section of employees. These employees, from their various perspectives within the company, could keep the staff informed about actual and potential changes in the workplace that might have an impact on the project. They could answer questions as they arose and help locate other information.

Supported through both formal and informal relationships, the Language Working partnership remained strong and highly visible. Because the company's support for the project was well known, the project had a legitimacy that made employees more willing to become involved and to provide access to information and observation. The visibility of the project meant that some individuals sought us out and volunteered their help. It was relatively easy to introduce new people to Language Working since most workers already shared a basic level of knowledge about the project.

Liberal Education for Work

By structuring a partnership that allowed input and direction from both education and industry, the Language Working project was able to achieve objectives associated with both the education for work familiar to industrial trainers and the liberal education familiar to university faculty. Although the contexts for learning associated with a training center and a college classroom at first appeared discrepant, the compatibility of their educational goals became apparent as the partners worked together on a specific instructional program. While abstract discussions may emphasize differences between vocational and academic education, applied work on a concrete learning situation revealed the commonality of the underlying skills required for success in both contexts.

The Language Working training program helped to develop the kind of worker that industry wants and liberal education promotes: an individual trained to communicate effectively, think critically, make decisions, and work as part of a team. The program emphasized the dynamic language skills required to cope with the changing nature of today's work environments. Worker-students learned strategies for adapting to change and for acquiring and imparting new knowledge.

Focusing on generic competencies necessary for creative work and independent learning, this context-specific, job-related program was consistent in goals with traditional liberal arts course work. The collaborative effort that went into developing the Language Working project refutes the current rhetoric decrying the increasing gap between education for work and liberal education. A single program can achieve the purposes of both if an effective partnership is first established.

Elizabeth F. Skinner is a faculty associate at the National Center for Postsecondary Governance and Finance at Arizona State University in Tempe, Arizona. The center's current research concerns the educational attainments of minority students in higher education.

Nancy A. Siefer is a doctoral candidate in the Division of Educational Leadership and Policy Studies at Arizona State University. She is currently a consultant in international education for the Maricopa Community Colleges of Maricopa County in Arizona.

Barbara A. Shovers is a doctoral candidate in adult education at Arizona State University. She is currently an instructor in English as a second language for Arizona State University and South Mountain Community College in Phoenix, Arizona.

New technical skills and applications are integrated within existing occupational programs to provide industry with graduates or retrained employees in high technology.

Developing a Computer-Integrated Manufacturing Education Center

Victor Langer

Hard hit by foreign competition and factory automation, Milwaukee industries are working collaboratively with the Milwaukee Area Technical College (MATC) to develop the cadre of technicians they will need to compete effectively in a manufacturing environment dominated by computer-aided design (CAD) and the flexible manufacturing cell (FMC). CAD and FMC are only a part of computer-integrated manufacturing (CIM), which permits the industry to minimize inventory and automate the manufacturing process. CIM demands a highly skilled labor force to keep the entire system functioning.

The Milwaukee Area Technical College gathered data about regional manufacturers concerning their labor needs and the technological skills required of employees. The result is that MATC has developed close working relationships with area employers. The college not only trains recent high school graduates but also provides a substantial program of retraining for those laid off by old-line industries as well as those fortunate enough to hold jobs in growing firms. Much of the equipment being used in the school has been donated by the industrial partners, and the firms help define the technology and curriculum used in MATC's program.

Finally, these firms evaluate the program and its graduates to make sure that the curriculum achieves the goals that have been set.

The program is designed around computer-based labs that simulate the operating environments in the industries in which the student will work. "Clearly, the people at MATC believe that the best way to teach people how to operate and maintain such systems is to put them in an environment much like they will be using later on and help them become proficient users of those systems. This sounds very much like Carnegie-Mellon's definition of computer literacy" (Tucker, 1983-84, p. 37).

The Need for the "Supertech"

A careful examination of scientific hardware and modern industrial processes reveals complex systems that may be composed of combinations of electrical, electronic, mechanical, pneumatic, hydraulic, thermal, and optical devices. The person who works with high-technology equipment and systems must have a broad technical background to deal effectively with a variety of technologies. The manufacturer's greatest need, then, is for the "supertech," who can install, operate, maintain, and repair systems that may incorporate combinations of electrical motors, digital circuits, mechanisms, hydraulic actuators, lenses, light sources, and transducers. Many of the systems are controlled by microcomputers and are part of huge computerized data bases that require operators skilled in information management, including documentation development, storage, retrieval, and decision making.

Persons with such interdisciplinary skills and knowledge do not just emerge. They must be prepared through well-designed programs that include the broad knowledge bases required to apply the needed interdisciplinary skills. These are the technicians that MATC prepares for industry.

A broad understanding of basic principles in the various functional areas of high technology guarantees that the technician has flexibility. Although jobs that are repetitive or hazardous probably will be performed in the future by industrial robots, this does not mean that the displaced worker will no longer be needed. The worker obviously knows more about the requirements and skills of that specific job than anyone else. Logically, then, the displaced worker may re-emerge as a "technical supervisor" of a crew of five or six industrial robots. Such workers can be promoted and upgraded if they are willing and able to retrain for the technical aspects of their new jobs. In the high-technology occupations, however, this means extensive retraining in broad technical principles and equipment. A six-week, "quick-fix" course on how a particular robot works is simply not sufficient to produce the technologically competent workers needed for America's future (Hull, 1982).

CIM Technology

The advantages of CIM technology must be examined in the context of the primary Milwaukee industrial base, which is that of durable-goods manufacturing. Specifically, Milwaukee is known for its high-quality, precision metal-working industry.

The need to automate became necessary for the survival of this industry, and thus, the need to train and retrain a work force in the science of automation and machining has become an imperative at MATC. CIM technology integrates business, engineering, and manufacturing functions and requires numerous occupational categories to support automation. The relationship of functions within the automated factory is shown in Figure 1.

Project Profile

In the Milwaukee area, the Society of Manufacturing Engineers (SME) encouraged MATC to develop automation training programs as the result of its forecast for the future of flexible manufacturing systems. In this forecast, SME has predicted that, by 1990, 50 percent of all process plants will be computer controlled.

In response, MATC developed the CIM project to integrate new technical skills and technological applications with existing occupational programs. For example, drafters now learn how to be CAD operators, and welders are taught robot programming skills.

The overall goal of the project is to provide industry with graduates and retrained employees who can embark on high-technology careers in computer-integrated manufacturing and information management, as well as to disseminate software and courseware through established networks. The specific objectives of the project design were to provide cost-effective solutions to high-technology education. Industrial partnerships, an open resource center for maximum scheduling of expensive student stations, microcomputers, emulation of costly industrial systems, and course work all contribute to the efficient use of the program's resources.

The project, supported by a three-year grant from the Fund for the Improvement of Postsecondary Education (FIPSE), is now accomplishing its overall goal. A brief look at how this success unfolded may be helpful for educational institutions trying to serve similar clients.

In the first year, the project staff emphasized the research of competencies and jobs needed in the computer-integrated manufacturing areas. The result was the establishment of a new curriculum entitled "Computerized Machining"; its purpose was to teach the managing, operating, and programming of automated machinery. The new curriculum required the renovation of the Electromechanical Program; this program was retitled

Figure 1. Computer-Integrated Manufacturing Relationships

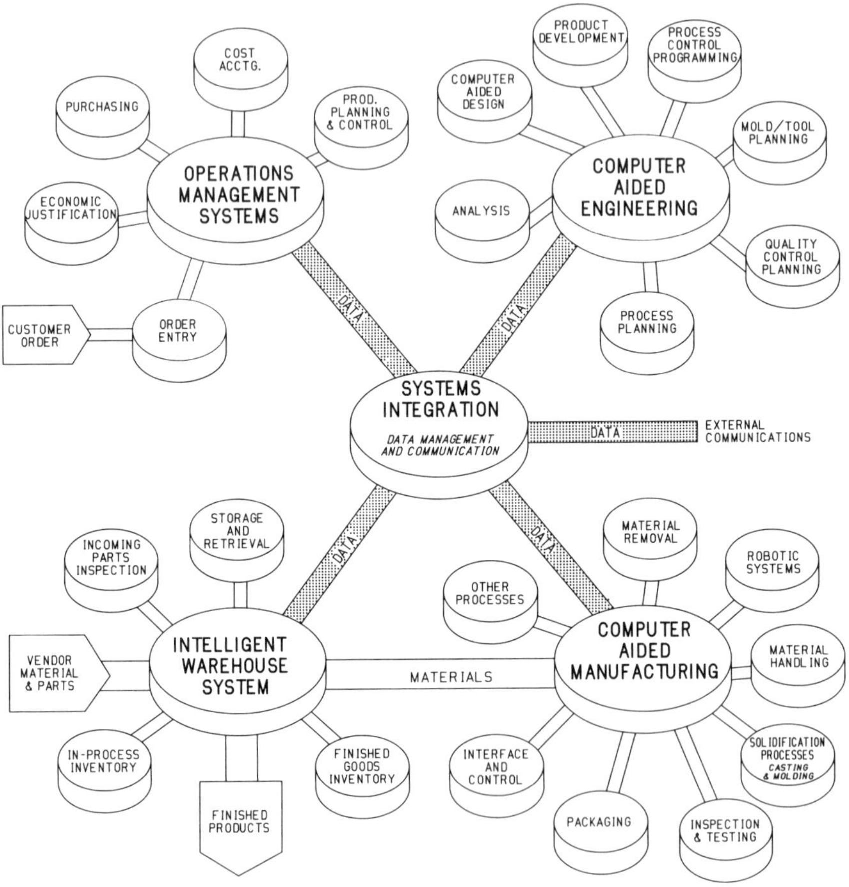

Source: James, 1985.

"Automated Manufacturing Technology," and it satisfies the training needs for installation and repair technicians of automated systems. In addition, industrial engineering, manufacturing engineering, and related industrial programs had to be altered and upgraded to meet the stringent requirements for those pursuing careers in CIM.

During the second year of the project, student groups completed first-year courses of the new and renovated programs. In the third year, the second-year students completed courses developed during the summer and the academic year.

To accommodate a complete flexible manufacturing cell, MATC undertook a major remodeling project, which called for the installation of $1.5 million in new machinery. This included the addition of two miniature automated manufacturing labs (AMLs). The mini-AML cells permit the teaching of concepts prior to the use of high-cost industrial systems. The minicells operate and use the same commands as the industrial FMC.

Partnerships were established with eleven corporations that agreed to help equip the FMC facility. These firms also volunteered technical support for developing both curriculum and facilities.

Course materials and personal-computer CAD/CAM software have been developed and are being refined for dissemination. A pilot national satellite television conference, "CAD/CAM: Are You Ready?," was broadcast on March 15, 1985, to sixty-seven sites and 2,500 participants. This broadcast involved MATC's Public Broadcasting Service (PBS) channels 10 and 36, the National Computer Graphics Association, and Sandia National Laboratories.

MATC's CIM project ended the development phase in December 1986. The first students have graduated and in the Spring 1986 semester, there were 207 students enrolled in the four primary programs under the project's auspices.

Perspectives on Project Success

CIM Technology Leadership at MATC. To a degree, MATC may be in advance of local industry, which has not generally installed CIM or cellular manufacturing. This is not unexpected, since MATC developed a model facility and curriculum in order to provide industry with a resource for technical guidance and retraining of the work force. The staff at MATC faced the same problems that industry faces in attempting to upgrade, including employee resistance to change, staff training, incompatible hardware and software, the high cost of installation and of staff, and especially the rapid turnover of staff.

Top-Level Support. The numerous and timely decisions necessary for the project's success demanded top administrative support. MATC's dean of the Technical and Industrial Division as well as the executive dean, chief executive officer, and the board of directors were all committed to providing the support and flexibility required by the project. The top-level assistance was needed to overcome the confusion of the bureaucratic maze, state contract laws, the budget process, and to meet important timetables and negotiate industrial partnerships. In addition, the commitment and support of the project team, comprised of industry consultants and MATC faculty and staff, was critical to meeting the rigorous timetable.

The Steering Committee. A steering committee was appointed to guide development of the project. Committee members included leaders in automation who represented the industries to be served by graduates and retrained employees. Representatives of labor unions, professional associations, high schools, and universities also served on the committee.

Significant factors in the project's success were the use of community leaders and the infrastructure of the committee itself. The committee was organized to establish subcommittees with the ability to add new members who had technical knowledge to contribute. The first subcommittees were to assess skill requirements in the following areas: (1) industrial engineering and manufacturing engineering, (2) automated manufacturing, (3) computer science, (4) computerized machining, and (5) welding technology.

The subcommittee chairpersons met as an overall curriculum committee that recommended and prioritized the needed areas of development for MATC. The curriculum committee presented the final report of recommendations to the steering committee at the end of the first year of the project. Priorities were also established for the second- and third-year activities that would implement the curricular changes.

Two additional subcommittees were established: procurement, to guide acquisitions of hardware and software, and industrial retraining, to guide employee retraining courses and programs within MATC.

The intense involvement of steering committee members with MATC staff created very positive working relationships, with the result that many of the companies donated technical support as well as hardware and software throughout the project.

Faculty Training and Selection. Faculty were given the opportunity to improve their skills in computers and automation techniques through workshops and courses taught by industrial adjunct faculty and by external consultants. Some MATC faculty attending vendor workshops returned to teach other faculty these newly learned techniques. Faculty selected to become involved in the project were in high-priority areas, had voluntarily obtained CAD training, had successfully developed curriculum materials, and had active industrial relationships.

Technology Leadership from Industry. One of the problems in establishing a program such as MATC's CIM is that the technology is so new and so much in demand that those most knowledgeable in the field are often pirated by others. MATC's solution to this problem was to reinforce its partnerships with industry. After the first year, MATC solicited technical support from leading local automation companies. Rexnord Industrial Automation Systems stepped forward to offer a project engineer on a half-time basis to coordinate the facility and curriculum. The FIPSE project provided the MATC salary match to Rexnord for the sixteen-month project engineer partnership.

The project engineer's first task was to review the facility requirements and redefine the cell specifications. The cell was defined as "world class" since it involved numerous vendor products and was thus typical of the manufacturing world. (A turnkey FMC operation available from some vendors with all the same controls and same-vendor products was ruled out in favor of this composite system.)

The second step was to negotiate with the different industrial vendors for partnerships providing both technical support and products. Several technical issues required the involvement of corporate vendor research offices in order to provide customized products. Rexnord became the prime contractor for developing the cell interface. Allen-Bradley donated a machine controller and the central programmable controller; ASEA donated a robot; CIMLINC donated a CIM workstation; Computervision donated software; Numeridex donated a graphic control system; Square D donated a programmable controller; and PREP, Inc., and Technovate, Inc., provided support in developing the minicells. Kearney-Trecker, Bridgeport, Enerpac, and Digital Equipment Corporation provided heavy discounts in equipment and software as well as technical support in application engineering and training. To date, over $2.2 million has been provided to MATC by its industrial partners.

Raising Performance Standards of MATC Graduates. On the advice of its curriculum committee, MATC adopted eight recommendations aimed at strengthening its CIM program:

1. Prerequisite compentency testing will be required for all entering students.

2. Students deficient in entrance skills are to be channeled into a pretechnical program.

3. The entrance mathematics requirement will be raised to the equivalent of Tech Math 1, permitting students in automated manufacturing to start in Tech Math 2 and also to complete a calculus course.

4. The new applied physics course will cover principles of physics, including the application of calculus.

5. MATC will strive to strengthen ties with industry by having faculty attend vendor training courses, by arranging student tours and student internships, by promoting joint development of CIM materials and software, and by inviting industry guest lecturers.

6. MATC will actively seek Accreditation Board for Engineering Technology (ABET) approval for its curriculum.

7. MATC will offer a common technical graphics course including

CAD, a common "Computer Programming for Technicians" course, and the applied physics courses.

8. A concept will be developed that integrates the economics of automation within the industrial automation course.

In addition, the "Computer Programming for Technicians" course is to be taught by mathematics faculty rather than electronics faculty. The industry representatives also recommended the addition of a technical writing course as a third semester of English. The curriculum committee wanted the program to prepare graduates with broad enough competencies so that they could be sent to vendor schools and have a high probability of success. The educational outcomes needed to succeed as an automated manufacturing technician were the ability to think effectively, to communicate, to judge, and to discriminate.

If the level of entering students is controlled and the level of instruction improved, then the quality of graduates will be improved. Thus, more jobs will be available to graduates. Students aggressively seek out successful career paths and usually find out where to go to get a quality education with a good chance of getting a good job. Therefore, even with raised entrance standards, more students will want to enroll because of job opportunities. This especially holds true for minorities (Langer, 1984).

Industrial Retraining and Continuing Education. With the development phase completed, the CIM project is now part of the MATC curriculum. Today, MATC offers 143 occupational programs to the community. Many students are employed full time and take programs on a continuing education basis.

Employees being retrained fall into three general categories:

1. Some are technicians or skilled workers learning application of new technology to current occupations, such as drafters or designers acquiring CAD skills or welders acquiring robotic programming skills.

2. Others are technicians or skilled workers preparing for new technician or skilled-worker occupations, such as a welder enrolled in the basic electronics program.

3. Others are unskilled workers seeking basic skills training, in areas such as shop math, metrology, and blueprint reading, as preparation for entering skilled areas.

Through traditional continuing education delivery mechanisms, including on-site contract training, MATC is helping facilitate the modernization of the local manufacturing and engineering industries (Langer, 1986). Strategies are being developed to arrange blocks of time for industrial retraining; these blocks of time would consist of two-hour lectures and two-hour hands-on experience sessions. In highly technical programs, specialized courses are occasionally offered late in the day or in the evening, with a client mix of full-time students and full-time employees. Often, advanced courses have only a few students, and the addition of worker retraining students can fill the section. When the worker shares his or her on-the-job experience in class, it helps prepare the full-time student for employment and provides an additional benefit.

Cost-Effective Delivery of High-Cost Workstations. MATC developed a CAD software package called MATC CAD to operate similarly to Computervision's industrial CAD system. MATC CAD currently is in use by more than 700 educational institutions. The initial cost of $100,000 per industrial workstation was reduced to less than $1,500 per MATC CAD personal computer (PC) based workstation including hardware and software. This very significant reduction makes CAD education affordable and practical.

Of particular benefit to educational systems that cannot afford the multimillion-dollar CIM cell, the same concepts may be presented through use of miniature low-cost tabletop components. A complete automated manufacturing lab consisting of mills, lathe, robots, conveyor, foundry, inspection, and cell computers using industrial commands is now packaged for tabletop use to cut wax or to cut metal at a fraction of the industrial cell cost of $1.5 million. The automation concepts can be taught in less space, for less capital investment, and less maintenance cost on the minicell.

Quality Elements for Integrating Education and Work

In summary, the key components, approaches, and practices essential for educational institutions to develop a quality high-technology program include:
1. *Faculty and staff:*
   - Lead faculty should have advanced degrees, occupational experience, additional specialized training, successful publication or leadership skills, and commitment to succeed.
   - Faculty assignments should be about half research and development and half teaching.
   - Technical support staff is needed to enhance faculty expertise and to maintain operations.
2. *Facilities and equipment:*
   - Facilities should be located in the "industrial base" of the program.
   - Facilities and equipment must reflect state-of-the-art industrial installations.
   - The vendors should provide continuous support in hardware, software, and application engineering (not necessarily without cost to institution).
3. *Curriculum and instruction:*
   - Technology should be integrated into the program as a "tool."
   - Concepts are stressed, rather than the language of technology.
   - Problem solving is stressed.

- Successful industrial retraining requires a mix of full-time students and experienced employees who are working to upgrade or advance their present skills.
4. *Business/industry cooperation:*
- Curriculum and procurement must be guided by a steering committee of industry representatives.
- The project engineer should be a key industry executive who can devote at least 50 percent of his or her time to college activities and 50 percent to industry activities.
- Donation of resources including development activities are essential to the creation of a world-class center.
- Faculty should be employed during the summer for four to ten weeks so that the members may gain relevant occupational experiences in an industrial setting.
5. *Budget, resources, and support:*
- Funds from grants enable the hiring of a technical "guru."
- Products developed having a market potential may be revenue generators as an entrepreneurial activity.
- Grants inspire a commitment to goals within a time frame normally not possible.
- Top-level administrative support is mandatory in order to maintain a commitment to aggressive goals.
6. *Student recruitment, selection, and support:*
- Linkages with industries and high schools provide students who are prepared and, in many cases, who may be enrolled with advanced standing.
- Prerequisites must be clear, and testing to qualify potentially successful candidates may be necessary. In some cases, candidates may be placed on a remedial track to help ensure success.
- The products should be disseminated to high schools. This will aid in attracting academically superior and motivated students.

References

Hull, D. *Preparing Students for High-Tech Careers.* Arlington, Va.: 1982.

James, C. F. "The Center for Integrated Manufacturing Processes and Controls." Proposal submitted to the National Science Foundation, University of Wisconsin, Milwaukee, September 3, 1985.

Langer, V. "Curriculum Subcommittee Report to the CIM Steering Committee." Unpublished paper, Milwaukee Area Technical College, Milwaukee, Wisconsin, 1984.

Langer, V. "Industrial Retraining Subcommittee Report to the Steering Committee." Unpublished paper, Milwaukee Area Technical College, Milwaukee, Wisconsin, 1986.

Tucker, M. S. "Instruction and the Computer." In M. S. Tucker (ed.), *Computers on Campus: Working Papers.* Current Issues in Higher Education, no. 2. Washington, D.C.: American Association of Higher Education, 1983-84.

Victor Langer is manager of instructional development, including academic computing, at Milwaukee Area Technical College. He is president of MATC CAD, an "intrapreneurial" software enterprise at the college, and is founder and board member of the Wisconsin Computer Graphics Association in Milwaukee, Wisconsin.

Comprehensive education services are adapted to the realities of emerging growth companies in a corporate park.

The Business Development and Training Center: An Educational Maintenance Organization

Lois Lamdin, Maxine Ballen Hassan

Today the Business Development and Training Center (BDTC) runs an education and training center in the largest corporate park in the East, provides a variety of academic and career counseling services, coordinates such disparate activities as a consultant file, the Career Connections Job Service, and numerous special-interest groups, and publishes a newspaper with a circulation of 12,000.

How did it start? What are the critical elements of the educational maintenance idea, and how does it become a reality? This case study provides the answers to these questions and explores what was learned about integrating education and work in the process of developing a new approach to education and human resource development.

The BDTC was a joint project of the Compact for Lifelong Educational Opportunities (CLEO) and the Great Valley Corporate Center in Malvern, Pennsylvania. The corporate center was developed by Rouse & Associates to be the "workplace of the future"; CLEO, on the other hand, was a consortium of postsecondary institutions in southeastern Pennsylva-

nia, which was created in order to attract and provide services for the new adult learner. CLEO's initial objectives were to:
- Attract adult learners back to further schooling through the use of print media, public service announcements on radio and television, and public information sessions in various sites around Philadelphia and the adjoining four counties
- Provide academic and career counseling, "hotline" information on courses and programs available in member institutions, and assessment of prior learning
- Provide faculty and staff development activities to support the kinds of change needed if adults were to be well served by higher education.

Built on the philosophy of the health maintenance organization, the educational maintenance organization (EMO) was initially conceived as creating an overall system of educational services and accountability to be shared by employers, unions, educational organizations, and individuals.

Taking the EMO idea as its basis, CLEO proposed to develop a model with the following distinguishing factors:
- On-going, on-site provision of a variety of training, counseling, and other services as needs arose
- Mutual commitment of educators and employers to supporting a multifaceted human resources program
- A financing structure in which corporations would prepay for services.

It was envisioned that, by contracting with CLEO, a company would have access to the teaching, research, and consultation capacity of thirty-four major colleges and universities, and they could thus shift some of the burden of human resource management and training to the educational maintenance organization. In this way, the colleges would gain the recognition and experience needed to reclaim their role as primary providers of educational services to the business world, and the learners would gain access to learning resources appropriate to achieving their personal and career goals.

The proposal to develop an EMO was financed by the Fund for the Improvement of Postsecondary Education (FIPSE). Today's Business Development and Training Center at Great Valley Corporate Center, while it adheres to the underlying principles of the EMO, bears only a superficial resemblance to the creature initially envisioned by those who wrote the FIPSE proposal.

The Business Development and Training Center

In the midst of Great Valley Corporate Center, where stunning contemporary buildings sprawl among the rolling hills of Chester County,

Rouse & Associates have preserved a late-eighteenth-century farmhouse. The first floor of the farmhouse has been renovated for the BDTC's use with an interesting mixture of colonial charm and twentieth-century functionalism. One fairly large space was turned into a classroom that can hold thirty-five to forty people. A conference room with a table seating ten to twelve remains a conference room, but, with extra chairs, it can seat up to twenty for a small class or workshop. Some open office space and a small room in the basement that can be used by part-time staff complete the BDTC headquarters.

Great Valley Corporate Center is marketed as the "workplace of the future," a high-tech park that serves as the hub of the emerging high-tech Route 202 corridor. The marketing hype has in fact created a reality, and there are now a large number of young, entrepreneurial companies in the center, creating a stimulating but volatile environment.

The average size of the companies in the center is very small. Of the 181 companies present in the spring of 1986 (that number has increased since), 140 had twenty or fewer employees, while only two companies had more than 250 employees. The center consists largely of high-tech and information services companies, with only 29 percent of the total in such traditional fields as sales and distribution, utilities, and light manufacturing. Sixty-two percent of the employees in the center are in the high-tech or biomedical/chemical/pharmaceutical and computer areas, and only 18 percent are in sales, distribution, and utilities.

On-Site MBA Program. By the spring of 1984, the BDTC had identified a core group of about thirty-five men and women who wanted to pursue a graduate degree in business but who were reluctant to enroll in an MBA program that would mean traveling into the city, fighting traffic and parking problems. They were eager to have an on-site program developed and were willing to help.

The first step was to invite the deans of the business schools of the major universities to meet with these potential students. Of the nine invitees, the deans of five schools attended. A second meeting with the potential students and the deans of the three most interested participating universities was followed by a period during which programs, faculty, tuition costs, and general attitudes were compared. Finally it was decided to invite St. Joseph's University to bring in its program. At every step of the way, the BDTC worked with and deferred to the judgment of the potential students, which not only made them feel more invested in the program but also saved the BDTC from charges of favoritism by the universities.

St. Joseph's University seized the opportunity to extend its reach into the corporate world. The university had already established two satellite campuses within a reasonable distance of Great Valley and was able to schedule classes in such a way that a student could be reasonably assured of being able to take most of the required courses without having to go to the city campus. St. Joseph's made arrangements with its bookstore for textbooks to be brought to the BDTC at the beginning of each semester.

The program's success has amply justified St. Joseph's leap of faith. There seems to be a steady stream of new and continuing degree candidates. There are enough students to justify two very well-filled courses per semester, for three semesters per year. The students are pleased with the quality of the program and the responsiveness of both faculty and administrators, and St. Joseph's reputation in the business community has received a substantial boost. The program has enhanced the BDTC's ability to meet the needs of the people in the Great Valley area and has raised its profile in the corporate world.

Other Courses, Workshops, and Seminars. After an agonizingly slow first six months, the BDTC's training and education programs began to take off. Initial problems were probably inevitable given its newness on the scene. Because of budgetary constraints, public relations efforts were inadequate, and, even among those who had heard of it, the BDTC was viewed as an unknown quantity with an imperfectly understood mission. Nearly two-thirds of the scheduled courses in those first six months had to be cancelled. Registrations gradually improved in the spring and summer of 1984, and by the fall the BDTC had fairly respectable registration numbers.

Although most of the education and training is currently occurring on the premises of the BDTC, custom-designed training is clearly an important part of its future. It has been asked to coordinate several programs, and the number of requests are increasing as the BDTC becomes better known. One such program put together for General Electric (GE) is a good example of the kinds of company-specific needs that custom-designed training can fulfill.

Within Great Valley Corporate Center, there is a relatively small branch of GE specializing in the design and manufacture of control mechanisms for electrical power systems. The company was experiencing problems with quality control, which they suspected had to do with the older workers on the line who were untrained in the newer electronics. However, they were forbidden by their union contract to test the workers to determine their skill levels.

The BDTC brought in Delaware County Community College, which designed a forty-two-week program in the newer electronics. Because the college, not the company, was in charge of it, testing was allowed, and ultimately twenty-two GE employees participated in the program. At the end of the course, when they learned that they could receive twelve to eighteen credits through assessment, eight of these employees, all men over fifty, decided to go back to school.

This proved to a win-win situation all around. GE had solved its quality control problem, the college had produced a program that enhanced its reputation and was financially rewarding, the BDTC gained credibility as a resource for setting up training programs, and the employees had both retained their jobs and increased their skills.

Early in the BDTC's first year, staff became aware of employees' need to meet people in other companies who shared their professional concerns. As part of its first steps toward assuming responsibility for activities beyond education and training, the BDTC supported the formation of special-interest groups, setting up the meetings, publicizing them, serving refreshments, and staffing them until they could stand on their own. Among the groups supported were:

1. Toastmasters—Many of the people in the park were finding that, as they assumed more responsibility in their companies, they were frequently asked to speak and felt unsure of their abilities. Toastmasters was one of the first groups to form and has been one of the most enduring.

2. Human Resources Managers—Although the smaller companies in the park typically don't have anyone who is formally charged with responsibility for human resources, there was a group of managers from the larger companies who felt a need to share with their peers. The human resource group meets about four times per year, sometimes to discuss a specific issue, sometimes to hear an outside speaker.

3. High-Technology Group—This group has subsequently been incorporated as the Pennsylvania Innovation Network (PIN), part of a national network, and continues to grow and expand its agenda.

4. Secretaries and Administrative Assistants Advisory Group—This is a group that functions as a support mechanism for its members and for the BDTC as well. The members of this group give valuable feedback on the needs and interests of this very important segment of the corporate population.

5. Investment Club—This group is affiliated with the National Association of Investment Clubs and is composed of people from many levels of corporate life who wish to learn how to invest in stocks more wisely.

6. Executive Roundtable—This group, comprised of chief executive officers, meets monthly to share issues, resources, and information. Topics discussed range from venture capital, to the impact of the new tax reform bill on business, to sales and marketing issues.

7. Business After Hours—This is less a group than a function. The BDTC arranges for one company per month to host a reception at which people can meet and business cards can be exchanged. The receptions are well attended and very popular.

8. Technical Managers Group—Formed at the request of a middle manager in a software company, the group has worked with a consultant who leads discussions on issues of common concern.

9. Sales and Marketing Group—This group meets for breakfast once a month, at which time one of the members presents his or her marketing strategies for criticism by the others.

Career and Academic Counseling. A key theme in the EMO concept is support for the individual's self-directed learning. Using the career and academic counseling resources of CLEO, the BDTC has brought a complete array of adult-learner support services to Great Valley employees. In the first two years of the BDTC, over 500 persons either received individual counseling, used the DISCOVER computer-assisted career counseling program, went through the program designed to assess prior learning, or took College-Level Examination Program (CLEP) tests at the farmhouse.

The following chart of BDTC activities provides a summary of services provided in years one and two:

	Year 1	Year 2
Number of participants in BDTC-sponsored programs	599	1,323
Number of credits earned in MBA program	0	294
Number of persons receiving academic or career counseling and testing	207	315
Number of referrals to colleges and universities	59	84
Number of consultant referrals	12	47
Number of miscellaneous services to business	63	750

The **Great Valley News.** In September 1984, the BDTC began publishing a monthly newspaper, printing 12,000 copies of over forty pages with more than twenty pages of ads and distributing it all along the Route 202 corridor.

The reason for the success of the *Great Valley News* is related to the reasons why BDTC's program has been moving toward business services that provide linkages.

The workplace is replacing the neighborhood, the church, and maybe even the golf course as the "community" for many people. But this community can be fragmented, uncaring, or even hostile. The much overused and abused word "networking" becomes increasingly important as traditional ties of family and friends grow more fragile. People in the business community need to be able to share experiences, resources, ideas, and strategies. The *Great Valley News* has helped form a community in which these things can happen. Readers learn what is going on in the new company that moved into the building across the way; they see pictures of themselves and their colleagues at a meeting; they learn about the softball league schedule and the MIT Enterprise Forum and the hotshot management consultant who might help them with their production problem. They find out about opportunities to meet their counterparts in special-interest groups, and they learn where are the best places in the neighborhood to get a good lunch.

Increased Private Sector Involvement

In September 1984, a shift occurred from the college-driven agenda for the BDTC to one that would be more responsive to the needs of the tenant companies in the corporate center. This shift had relatively little to do with the fact that the BDTC was largely supported by Rouse & Associates. Instead, the shift evolved from a growing awareness of how the original mission could be modified to respond to new needs and new opportunities.

Given the genesis of the BDTC under the aegis of the Compact for Lifelong Educational Opportunities, it was perhaps natural to have assumed that the colleges and universities would be the sole purveyors of training and education at the BDTC. However, quite early on it became clear that the business sector itself was replete with expertise of all kinds that the experts themselves were willing and even eager to share.

The first real understanding of the important role that the private sector could play came when a group representing two major and highly respected legal and accounting firms and a large bank approached the BDTC directors with the suggestion that they put together an executive seminar series. Clearly it was in their interest to do so. The small companies in the corporate park represent potentially important future clients, and they could establish an early relationship with them through presenting the seminars.

The executive seminars became the BDTC's most notable success. The firms organized them around current issues about which they had firsthand information: copyright laws and software; how to cope with new tax regulations; going public; 401-K pension plans; and so on. They were scheduled for 5:00 to 6:30 in the afternoon once a month, wine and cheese were served, and the atmosphere was relaxed and collegial. The BDTC gained valuable visibility, a reputation for quality programming, and a modest profit as well. Clearly the colleges had strong competition.

The business community has been supportive of the BDTC in other important ways. A group of young business people who wanted to bring the MIT Enterprise Forum to the Delaware Valley asked it to staff and coordinate the project as well as take care of the mailings and registration. There are ten meetings per year, and the BDTC is reimbursed for services plus a generous amount for administrative overhead.

The president of a software company has offered to help develop a program to support the BDTC recruiting venture, Career Connections, and will lend the hardware on which to run it. The president of an energy company has given free warehouse space for the *Great Valley News;* the Rouse organization has helped with public relations; and everyone wants to give free advice.

Lessons Learned

The two and a half years of planning, development, and operation of the BDTC have been an exciting and frequently frustrating time, but certainly they have been a time of learning. This new educational services model, created in the high-minded naîveté of the academic world, has had to make a myriad of adjustments to the reality of corporate America. Among the lessons learned are these:

1. There is no question that the need for training and retraining in this transitional economy is enormous, perhaps exceeding the capacity of educational institutions to respond fully. However, in most small and many medium-sized companies, managers do not perceive that need, are paying it little attention, or simply cannot afford to do anything about it. It is in the larger companies that most training takes place or is supported by means of tuition reimbursement. Unless some way is found to aggregate the needs and resources of the smaller companies (through a BTDC or a chamber of commerce or some other cooperative model), this situation is unlikely to change.

2. There is less support for training for blue-collar workers unless such support is written into union contracts. The assumption seems to be that blue-collar workers are not (and should not be) upwardly mobile. In fact, the pressures of high-tech manufacturing and production techniques fall heavily on the blue-collar workers, and it is the blue-collar jobs that are most in jeopardy as we go through this transition to an information and service economy.

3. There is a demand for noncredit on-site courses, workshops, and seminars to which many colleges have been slow to respond. The demand is frequently not for off-the-shelf offerings but for a course tailored to meet a specific need. And when a company is experiencing a need, it does not want something promised six months later, after the curriculum committee has met and the academic dean has approved it and when the faculty person has a lighter schedule; it wants the need met now.

4. There is in the business world much skepticism about what colleges have to offer. They have a stereotype (sometimes accurate) about courses that are out of touch with the realities of the contemporary business world, taught by faculty who treat adult students as though they were nineteen years old and wet behind the ears. They see much that is irrelevant, dated, and impractical in the content and much that is a waste of time in the process. This set of perceptions is hard to overcome and means that much time must be spent by the educators in building credibility.

Implications for Integrating Postsecondary Education and Work

1. Any postsecondary institution interested in doing business with business should first look to its mission and its resources to determine if this is really a priority and if it has the appropriate programs, faculty, and administration necessary for its success.

2. Colleges should choose only their *best* faculty to teach off site and should make certain that they *want* to do it. Unwilling faculty make terrible teachers. Adult learners tend to be fair but highly critical. They recognize and will not stand for poorly prepared or out-of-date material, or for a condescending or inept pedagogical style.

3. Colleges must be prepared to be reasonably flexible when modifications of content or delivery are requested.

4. Colleges should be candid about what they cannot do. They should not take on contracts that will stretch their staff resources, compromise their academic integrity, or cause more dissension on campus than they are worth.

5. Colleges should look beyond course delivery to see what other resources they have to offer. A few colleges have begun to offer on-site career counseling or prior-learning assessment workshops. Others have done well with "Returning to Learning" seminars or simply by putting an academic counselor into an industrial plant a few days every year. An institution's relationship with the business community should not be just a series of courses. The institution should be thinking beyond courses to cooperative research projects, faculty-executive exchanges, internships, or consulting arrangements.

Relationships between the postsecondary education and business communities are a two-way street. Business does not have all of the money; colleges do not have all of the expertise. Both sectors are looking for rewards. They must work out win-win situations in order to build the foundation for true partnerships that are ongoing and mutually supportive. The EMO concept and its application through the BDTC show that education and work can be integrated to the benefit of all.

Lois Lamdin is codirector of the Business Development and Training Center at Great Valley Corporate Center in Malvern, Pennsylvania, and mid-Atlantic regional executive officer for the Council for Adult and Experiential Learning (CAEL).

Maxine Ballen Hassan is codirector of the Business Development and Training Center at Great Valley Corporate Center in Malvern, Pennsylvania.

"Economic literacy" curricula are designed for rank-and-file union members to enhance industry competitiveness and ease the processes of transition.

Worker Education for a Changing Economy: New Labor-Academic Partnerships

Charles Derber

Between 1983 and 1986, under a grant from the Fund for the Improvement of Postsecondary Education, a team of faculty and advanced graduate students from Boston College developed a new educational partnership with labor unions in Massachusetts to help combat problems of industrial dislocation and upheaval. In collaboration with the Massachusetts AFL-CIO, the Boston College group worked, over the three-year period, with five different union locals experiencing serious problems associated with foreign competition and new technology. The affected industries were in both manufacturing and service; they included locals of the International Ladies' Garment Workers' Union (ILGWU), the United Auto Workers (UAW), the International Union of Maritime and Shipbuilding Workers of America (IUMSWA), the American Federation of Teachers (AFT), and the Service Employees International Union (SEIU).

The project grew out of a long-standing interest by faculty in the Social Economy and Social Justice Program of the Boston College Sociology Department in helping fashion new economic and social responses to problems of job loss in core industries and of structural shifts and technological change in the economy. The Social Economy and Social Justice Program is committed to a vision of a democratic economy based on prin-

I. Charner, C. A. Rolzinski (eds.). *Responding to the Educational Needs of Today's Workplace.*
New Directions for Continuing Education, no. 33. San Francisco: Jossey-Bass, Spring 1987.

ciples of self-management. Its emphasis is on engaging workers, with their unions, in actively developing a response to the tremors shaking their industries and in creating a secure economic future for themselves. This implies a departure from the traditional pattern that assigns to management the power and responsibility for strategic economic planning, industrial development, and revitalization. This pattern relegates workers and their unions to a largely passive role, buffeted by management decisions and confined to a position of reaction rather than proactive participation and planning. Yet experience from other countries, such as Japan, West Germany, Sweden, and Yugoslavia, suggests that, when workers are included in the planning process, they can contribute substantially to the design of new industrial strategies for enhancing industry competitiveness and smoothing the painful processes of transition.

The Boston College project, then, arose from the view shared by both concerned faculty and top labor officials in Massachusetts that workers need to play an active role in the effort to preserve and revitalize local industries. This requires, among many other deep-seated changes, a new model for labor education, and this was the specific need that our project intended to address. Workers desperately need access to many kinds of knowledge currently reserved for management: knowledge about their own industry and the nature of the new global production and market, information about national and regional economic trends, understanding of new technological developments and the kinds of skills likely to be in demand both in their own and in other industries, and education for social and economic planning and development. This kind of "economic literacy," a precondition for worker self-management and for a proactive labor movement, is not a significant part of any of the prevailing models of labor education, largely because these models accommodate the existing structure of industrial relations.

The project was conceived explicitly as an experimental, highly innovative, labor education model that could demonstrate both the possibilities and the payoffs of providing workers and unions with a tailored "economic literacy" program focusing on the current problems of their own industries. The concept was radically distinct from traditional retraining programs, since our concern was not to provide technical training for specific jobs but rather a kind of social, historical, and economic education that would give workers the tools to formulate strategies for charting their own economic future and would help them analyze, revitalize, or retool their own industries. Among the assumptions of our model were (1) the need for a *new partnership* between universities and labor federations committed to providing to labor many of the analytical tools and forms of information traditionally offered to managers and (2) the need for a *new critical social curriculum* that would stretch labor's sense of its capacities and rights to chart its own economic destiny.

Our location in Massachusetts might seem anomalous, given the widespread perception that Massachusetts has prospered, escaping the economic anguish of the Midwest and many of the other northeastern industrial states. Yet, while Massachusetts has done well in terms of aggregate performance and the strength of many of the high-technology industries, as well as in terms of the academic and financial sectors, many local manufacturing industries have experienced severe loss of jobs and capital. There have been plant closings, extensive job loss, and underemployment in the apparel and shipbuilding industries, two of those selected by the project. In addition, we selected the major automobile assembly plant in the state because its position is threatened as the auto industry both retrenches domestically to the Midwest and goes overseas. Some of the public sector has been thrown into upheaval by demographic change, budgetary austerity, and technological changes, with significant job loss among teachers and municipal service workers; thus, we chose to work with both of these worker categories as well.

Initially, we hoped to apply a relatively uniform approach to all locals. The approach would involve collection of relevant information about the particular region and industry, preparation of an "economic literacy" curriculum tailored to the particular plant, and holding of educational forums in union halls for staff and members where information could be made easily accessible in a familiar and unthreatening location. The central labor federation helped us gain access to the locals and work sites. Faculty and graduate students prepared the relevant information and curricula, based both on research and interviews with local managers, workers, and state officials, and then taught forums in the union setting. We also hoped to help institutionalize educational committees in each local that would continue this educational program once our project ended. The actual projects, as described below, varied from this template as required by individual circumstances, but we have carried out research, prepared "economic literacy" curricula, and taught forums or seminars in each of our local sites as conceived in our initial model.

Initiating the Project

The cooperation necessary to create the Boston College–AFL-CIO partnership started with the project itself. Project faculty had no prior contact with state labor leaders, although we had relations with some labor organizers and local leaders. One local leader who liked the idea of the project arranged a meeting with top state labor federation officials. It was in this meeting that a cooperative program crystallized. The president and secretary-treasurer of the Massachusetts AFL-CIO recognized the severity of the problems faced by manufacturing industries, for they had been involved in plant closings and were members of state commissions con cerned with the declining fortunes of basic industries in the state. The project offered them an opportunity to demonstrate to their members their commitment to the jobs issue, and it offered new resources for their own office staff (the project coordinator worked primarily out of the AFL-CIO office). The coordinator was our liaison with the labor community and demonstrated to locals that this was a project endorsed and sponsored by their own top state officials. The full-time coordinator role was critical, for it provided a connection between two partners who were relative strangers. It allowed the AFL-CIO to experience ownership of the project, while providing the academics with access to locals that would otherwise have been unavailable to them. The coordinator was selected by the AFL-CIO as someone who had both experience in the labor movement and the necessary educational background to carry out the role. Faculty interviewed and confirmed the AFL-CIO choice.

Two Projects: A Success and a Failure

Each local project was a minipartnership between the Boston College staff and the local union leadership. A faculty member, one or more graduate students, and the coordinator constituted a "team," such as the "garment team" or the "auto team," to work with the relevant local. Each team was responsible for completing research on the industry, preparing the curricula, and teaching the forums. Brief descriptions of two local projects, one that succeeded and one that failed, are provided in the following subsections.

The ILGWU. The partnership with the International Ladies' Garment Workers' Union was the first and one of the most successful of the local projects. The "garment team" consisted of an advanced graduate student in sociology, a faculty member, and a respected representative of the regional ILGWU office, who was strongly committed to education and whose support proved of great importance to the project's success. The team spent almost a year carrying out an intensive study of the problems of the garment industry in the southeastern part of the state, centered in Fall River. The industry had been in decline and had been losing jobs to foreign competition for many years. With access facilitated by the AFL-CIO and the ILGWU representative, the team was able to enter many small firms in the area, interview numerous workers and owners, and talk to local municipal officials and trade association personnel, as well as local college administrators. On the basis of this in-depth research, the team prepared a detailed report for the union, involving specific recommendations for a strategy of job stabilization and worker education. The report pointed to the need for a cooperative union-management resource center, which would help the industry develop a coherent and stable production and marketing plan, coordinate its chaotic and underemployed labor market, and create new educational opportunities for workers. The educational opportunities would enable workers to understand their industry and would help them develop multiple skills rather than competence in only one narrow task, such as making buttonholes.

The garment team presented its information to the union in several forums. Two presentations were made to the union executive board, which consists of more than 100 workers. Extensive information about the industry and its work force and about the nature of its national and international competitive environment was presented graphically, along with the recommendations for change included in the report. At the same time, two-part workshops on the same subjects were offered to rank-and-file members at the union hall.

The team had become a familiar and trusted presence in the union, and its report received serious attention. Initially, there had been resistance because the union had defined its problem simply as governmental failure to provide adequate import protection. As a result of the project's research and dialogue with union officials and with the rank and file, union members began to see that there were other important facets of the problem. Concerned with the internal structure and management of the industry, they and their managerial counterparts committed themselves to follow through on a new industrial and educational strategy. On the basis of its report and seminars, the team was encouraged to prepare a grant that would create the proposed resource center and educational opportunities for workers. A $200,000 proposal was funded by the state to assist the local industry's employers and workers in developing new local strategies for job stabilization and for worker education and involvement.

The Shipbuilders. Despite innovative research and educational work in a large and fascinating industrial setting, the partnership with the International Union of Maritime and Shipbuilding Workers of America failed in its ultimate mission. The project was an effort to help provide the local maritime union at the gigantic General Dynamics Fore River Shipyard, located in Quincy, Massachusetts, with the knowledge and educational resources to cope with the threat of extreme cyclical unemployment, technological change, and severe decline in the domestic shipbuilding industry. Due to stiff Asian and domestic competition, the Quincy yard faced possible extinction. The project's objectives were to provide the local union with knowledge about the radically changing state of their industry and, through educational forums with stewards and workers, to help equip them for further training, participation, and the new role in management, product development, and marketing that characterized the most competitive yards.

The project had auspicious beginnings: It received an enthusiastic welcome from the local union president, a young progressive leader with strong interests in labor education and a clear recognition of the need for new directions in the union. Two staff members of our project, both advanced graduate students in sociology, spent several months preparing an in-depth analysis of the global and domestic shipbuilding industry; they also carried out intensive surveys of workers in each of the yard's major departments concerning its technical and organizational problems. The analysis and the survey results were compiled into a report about the industry and the yard, and this report served as the basis of several educational forums with the union's executive board and its stewards.

Unfortunately, this educational work did not lead to the kinds of continuing education and organizational change that would help the union and the yard survive. Major internal and external events frustrated our ongoing efforts, leading to no major changes in union policy and no deep commitment to the educational process that had begun. On the one hand, political divisions within the union overwhelmed its capacity to act concertedly in a new direction. The president had an uneasy relationship with some important groups in the union and ultimately resigned, placing the project under the sponsorship of a new president. The divisive political climate was not conducive to our continued presence and work. Although we established a relationship with the new leaders, it was not possible to carry on a sustained, innovative educational program that would have the full commitment and support of the union.

The press of external events also overwhelmed our efforts. In less than two years from our initial contact, the position of the yard had become untenable, with the completion of a major project and failure to win any new major navy or commercial contracts. In 1985, General Dynamics closed the yard, terminating the jobs of several thousand employees.

Other Projects

Projects with other unions have gone forward with varying degrees of success. Work with the Boston teachers' union has helped the union develop an educational program on the social and technical implications—for teachers, students, and the process of education itself—of the increasing use of computers in the schools. A project team is working with the Service Employees Union in Boston to implement a skills assessment, development, and training program for union members whose career mobility seems blocked in city hospital and other municipal settings. For two years, the project has also worked with a United Auto Workers local on the broad kinds of technical, economic, and organizational knowledge its members will require to keep their assembly plant competitive in the new global auto market and to preserve their own jobs in the face of rapidly spreading robotics and computer technology.

Lessons Learned

The project experience confirms that unions now need new forms of knowledge to survive. Traditional labor education on the nuts and bolts of collective bargaining, the grievance procedure, and enforcement of the contract remains important but far from adequate. As the viability of their industries is put to the test, unions must assimilate a broad range of economic, managerial, and sociological knowledge along with new technical skills. Our experience suggests that unions, under auspicious circumstances, will recognize the need for such training and participate actively in innovative programs.

A primary lesson learned is that the unions must play a role in the development of these innovative curricula. Workers themselves are the repositories of much of the knowledge required to understand their changing industries and jobs and of the strategies required to save them. Worker education for "economic literacy" not only means transmitting ideas and information from economics and other social science disciplines but it also means helping workers crystallize and pull together their own observations and insights about how their industry is being transformed, and it means facilitating their own process of developing options for themselves and their union.

Workers and their unions in declining or rapidly changing industries are understandably distrustful of outsiders, including academics, who claim to have knowledge relevant to their predicament. It is their jobs rather than those of the educators that are on the line. They instinctively look to trusted union brothers and sisters in the same boat rather than to those who have not shared either their experience or the risks they face.

Worker education for "economic literacy," then, must be especially sensitive to matters of trust, participation, and politics. We found it essential to develop close and relaxed working relations with influential union officials before we embarked on the joint design of educational programs for their members. The development of these relationships requires far more time and patience than we had anticipated—often more than a year simply to establish the requisite trust.

Substantial time is required as well for any outsider to get the "lay of the land" both within the union and the plant and in the industrial environment in general. Educators need to understand the political currents and alliances within the local unions, for example, in order to know what kinds of issues are salient and which issues are so divisive as not to be viable for presentation and discussion. It is also critical for educators working with local unions to identify key individuals capable of mobilizing broad support within the union for new programs. We developed important relations with "internal sponsors" in our more successful projects; these sponsors could help steer us through delicate political problems and find ways to build interest and support for educational programs in unions that had not previously sponsored or been involved in them.

We found it difficult in all the locals to mobilize serious commitment to these new educational endeavors. This reflected the press of other demands on staff, distrust of academics and higher education, and organizational inertia. Innovative educators must find ways of framing their "curricula" around problems already understood by the union as critical. In our garment project, this meant tying our forums concerning the internal organization of the industry to issues of government trade policy that already engaged the union. Educators have to be flexible in their presentation of ideas and learn to promote new curricula in ways that appeal to the existing thought and agenda of local unions.

Both educators and unions must experiment with new relations and programs, facilitated by "educational brokers" such as FIPSE. Another model showing great promise is that developed by the joint UAW-GM Human Resource Center in its Paid Educational Leave program for auto workers. Mandated and funded by provisions in the latest contract, the Human Resource Center has sponsored the development of an "economic literacy" and "governmental process" curricula for local UAW officials throughout the country. This program seeks to do on a national level for one union what we have tried to accomplish on a smaller scale for selected local unions in Massachusetts. The UAW program has brought in well-known academics, government leaders, and experts to help shape a highly innovative and sophisticated union-oriented curriculum for understanding the governmental process, the international economy and the changing position of the U.S. auto industry, the changing character of industrial relations, and new roles and options for unions. The Human Resource Center is now experimenting with pilot programs to carry forward this project at selected local plants with rank-and-file members.

Conclusion

Reaching the rank and file with programs of this sort is the greatest challenge for continuing educators. It requires close working relations between educational institutions and local unions, as well as a willingness by educators to adapt both their traditional curricula and their pedagogical style. The curricula for these programs must be developed through close consultation between academics and union officials and members. Courses should in many cases be held in the union hall rather than on the campus.

Long-term development of such programs wil require new partnerships between postsecondary institutions and local and state labor federations. Our project was possible only because of the sponsorship provided by the Massachusetts AFL-CIO. Problems of access, trust, logistics, and politics would never have been resolved without a close working relationship between the Boston College staff and an AFL-CIO coordinator. Bridging the unfamiliar terrain between colleges and labor organizations requires investment of resources and commitment to the endeavor that neither postsecondary institutions nor unions have shown until now. The present problems facing the economy may provide the incentive for both to get down to the new pressing educational tasks at hand.

Charles Derber is associate professor of sociology at Boston College in Boston, Massachusetts, and director of its graduate program in social economy and social justice.

Both content and method are designed and adapted to the learning environments of rural communities, with the focus on the use of the computer as a tool.

Computer Education Opportunities for Rural Adults

Mary Emery

Technology is likely to have a great impact on rural communities; rural people, however, often lack the resources to learn about technology. The Rural Education/Adult Development in Idaho (READI) project offers a unique approach to teaching rural adults about computers. The READI project is designed to provide access to computer literacy for adults who live where such opportunities are otherwise unavailable. The pilot for the project was financed by the Fund for the Improvement of Postsecondary Education and the Idaho Cooperative Extension Service in cooperation with the University of Idaho. During the pilot study, the project developed and tested a curriculum, designed a method of training people to use that curriculum, and tested a community-based delivery system. In less than three years, over 600 adults have enrolled in READI classes in fourteen rural locations. The project has also had a significant effect on elementary and secondary education in many of these areas.

Need for the Project

The READI project was developed not only because of the demand for computer education in rural areas but also because of the concern that rural areas with no access to computer training will continue to be left behind in this age of new technology. Opportunities to learn about computers are important to both individuals and to communities. Such opportunities are particularly important for those areas where the traditional rural industries are no longer able to support large portions of the population. Programs that foster the development of computer-related skills among rural adults can be vital resources in such communities. For instance, efforts in both job creation and economic development in these areas are likely to be related to new technology and to require employees who are already computer literate. In addition, the computer-literate consumer is increasingly important to the smooth flow of business as more and more establishments add computerized customer services. The role of computers in their children's education has encouraged many adults to narrow the generation gap by becoming computer literate. Finally, many rural adults seek educational opportunities in computers simply because of the fascination they have for the new technology.

Access to computer literacy programs is not the only problem rural adults face. Often, even when such programs do exist, they do not meet the needs of the students. For example, many existing courses focus exclusively on programming or on learning a specific software package. Teachers often assume that students have high levels of verbal and math skills, an assumption that results in many people dropping out. Those who do finish are often unable to use what they have learned because they do not know how to apply that knowledge to existing job and home situations. What is needed is a class that can acquaint adult learners with the computer and its uses as a tool for decision making and information management without making assumptions about verbal and math skills. The READI approach to computer literacy has been designed to provide a relevant and useful introduction to the computer and to computer applications by focusing on the computer as a tool.

The goals of the project were to develop an effective and appropriate curriculum and to pilot a cost-effective delivery mechanism for that curriculum. During the first year of the project, the curriculum was developed and the test sites selected. During the second year, we tested and modified the curriculum. In addition, the READI State Advisory Board began working on suggestions for making the project self-sufficient at the county level. During the third year, we offered the program at additional sites, completed the project evaluation design, and disseminated the project to other areas.

The READI Approach to Computer Literacy

The READI approach to computer literacy is multifaceted. The goal of providing computer literacy is coupled with an understanding of the need for basic skills review, practice in problem solving and decision making, and work or education referral information. READI also emphasizes an appreciation for rural values and life-styles, and the curriculum is learner centered; it focuses attention on the needs and concerns of the specific students it serves. Finally, since education does not take place in a vacuum, the READI project is designed to address implications for the future and to enhance critical-thinking skills so that rural adults may play a more proactive role in the information age.

An educational program designed to bring computer literacy to rural areas must address the factors that prevent rural adults from entering the computer age. Access is, of course, a critical factor because many rural people live too far from existing educational programs, and these programs have neither the resources nor the expertise to conduct courses in more isolated areas. Further, these rural communities cannot by themselves provide educational opportunities for their residents. These external factors can be overcome. The READI project provides a model for using local resources and expertise in developing low-cost courses in computer education for adults.

Such internal factors as poor esteem, lack of basic skills, math anxiety, and inadequate communication skills also prevent rural adults from taking advantage of whatever educational opportunities may exist. Local ownership and control of the program tend to break down such barriers for adults who want to attend computer courses. The READI curriculum has been designed to include activities that foster self-esteem and encourage self-motivation as well as those that review basic skills.

The READI curriculum design is intended to enhance problem-solving and decision-making skills, as well as to teach people about computers. Actual class activities are designed with two principles in mind. The first principle is that adults learn best by doing, particularly with activities that have a direct application to some part of their lives. For hands-on activities to be successful, however, the instruction must go beyond drill and practice and must involve the students in the discovery of knowledge. Such activities will also help participants to retain what they have learned and to integrate new knowledge more easily into everyday life.

The second principle is that interaction among peers can provide a very effective context for learning. Participants increase each other's understanding and self-confidence by sharing feelings and successes, by comparing problems and solutions, and by teaching each other. Since one of the goals of READI is to provide a learning experience that empowers participants to take hold of new opportunities, it is essential that the courses provide a setting where ideas can be exchanged and individual goals can be enhanced.

In short, neither content nor method in the READI curriculum represents a technical approach to providing computer literacy; rather, READI approaches computer literacy from a problem-solving focus with an emphasis on group interaction. The design reflects the recognition of a variety of types of expertise and of the need to share information in a meaningful way so that learning is both an exciting experience and a new discovery.

Using the computer in problem-solving situations also provides an opportunity to review basic skills. Since many rural adults did not finish high school, had an inadequate high school experience, or simply have allowed their basic skills to become rusty, it is desirable to provide some review and instruction of these skills. We cannot produce computer-literate adults without also dealing with illiteracy in other basic areas. While the READI course is not a substitute for an adult basic education or high school equivalency program, the curriculum has been written with attention to this need. Thus, reviews of math and writing skills necessary for specific types of problems are included. Clearly, if we are to empower adults by helping them become computer literate, we must address those skills that help individuals to write correctly, to estimate answers, and to use correct formulas.

For example, participants can review their math skills using the computer in small groups both to solve word problems and to construct them. While doing complicated math problems on computers, some using a spreadsheet and others using the computer in immediate mode, students can see how attention to order of mathematical operations is essential for effective computer use. During this class session, instructors also discuss the importance of estimation skills for computer users, and they provide instruction and practice time for students to work with estimating answers that they can then check on the computer.

Just as teaching someone how to use a hammer or a sewing machine involves much more than just teaching them how the tool works, providing computer literacy courses also means teaching students how to apply the computer as a tool. The READI approach focuses on common situations such as family budgets and mailing lists in order for students to learn how to apply the computer's power. In addition to these common applications, each participant is encouraged to apply a variety of computer tools to situations in his or her own life. In previous READI classes, for example, a small-town government clerk experimented with putting her records on a data base, a number of people looked at keeping their small-business records on data bases, and teachers made electronic record books.

In summary, the READI approach to computer literacy includes the following:

- Examining the social, political, and economic impact of computers on the future of individuals, communities, and the larger society

- Reviewing the skills necessary to apply the computer as a tool, including problem solving, decision making, math, writing, and information organization
- Helping participants gain confidence in using the machine by teaching computer terminology and basic programming skills
- Creating an opportunity for participants to learn how to manipulate and use data as well as to understand how computers store and use data
- Empowering individuals to make more informed decisions about their future and the role of computers in that future.

Preparing the Teachers of READI

The week-long READI Summer Institute prepares teachers to present classes in computer literacy. Many people interested in opportunities for adults to learn about computers overcome their reluctance to offer such courses when they have an already-developed curriculum and an opportunity to see how the class sessions work. At the institute, selected activities are modeled for participants so that they can see how the activities flow together. Additional time is spent learning about the problem-solving approach to teaching computer skills, about working with adult learners, and about setting up a READI class. Finally, each institute Fellow has an opportunity to develop a lesson plan using READI materials and to present it to the group. This exercise gives everyone a chance to learn from the different presentations and to get feedback on their style. Additional creative ideas are generated and shared in these sessions.

Making READI Available to Rural Adults

The READI project has been successful because it provides for maximum flexibility. It also places some of the responsibility, as well as some of the risk, on the rural communities themselves. READI provides an opportunity to expand local expertise and resources in both computer-related activities and leadership development. In Idaho, READI became one of several volunteer-run projects in the rural counties. The same method of organization could be used for other continuing education or community education programs.

The READI project has been developed on the assumption that local communities or county committees will take responsibility for running the project on the local level. University extension or continuing education programs share responsibility by providing additional expertise, help with networking, and access to a support person. This arrangement of shared responsibility and risk results not only in a program with local ownership and control but with expanded resources.

READI community advisory groups are organized to oversee the READI project on the local level. They play a vital role in the program's success. The committee is an essential link in the transition from a generic statewide project to an effective local program. The committee oversees the selection of local peer teachers, handles the logistics of setting up the program, and recruits the participants. In addition to adapting READI to local needs and resources, the committee participates in evaluating the project's successes and problems. The committee is also responsible for developing useful and up-to-date referral information for READI participants. By researching opportunities, the committee helps READI participants not only to see the READI experience as a stepping-stone to other activities but also to use the acquired skills in making a contribution to the community. The advisory committee uses the experiences of READI participants and their own knowledge of the community to plan future directions for the project in their location.

In addition to administering the programs at the local level and developing relationships with local resource people, the community advisory committee is also charged with developing a strategic vision of how technology will influence the area and with implementing strategies for maximizing the positive impact of technological change. Since rural areas are known for the way they cherish traditional values, the committee must mediate between the need for constancy within the community and the press for change. For each community, as with each individual, this balance is unique. What is acceptable in one area may not work in another. The READI approach provides for flexible schedules and program design, allowing classes to differ from community to community. The local committee monitors the success of the courses based on local criteria; the central office or support person monitors the quality of the instruction.

The actual classes are facilitated or taught by peer teachers, chosen not only on the basis of their understanding of computers but also because of their involvement with adults and their interest in educational or job-training activities. These peer teachers receive training in teaching computer literacy to adults at the READI Summer Institute.

By providing resources to local people, the project helps to foster local expertise, both in computer education and in leadership development. The READI project is, at heart, a grass-roots program encouraging active and meaningful participation by everyone in all aspects of the program. Part of the success of the project has been the development of local ownership in the program and, hence, local investment in its success. Developing local leadership skills in the planning and development of programs and in computer technology allows communities to make better decisions related to the impact of new technology and to apply this expertise to local conditions and concerns.

Developing Partnerships with Others

The READI project is essentially a partnership between an educational institution and community groups. Over 600 rural adults have enrolled in READI classes, and an additional 250 have participated in READI-sponsored community computer expositions. We estimate that forty kindergarten through twelfth-grade teachers have used READI materials in their classes, affecting approximately 2,000 students.

READI has also had an impact on the communities in which it has offered classes. Two counties, for example, completed a survey of computer use in their area. Two other counties have developed community education or continuing education programs for rural learners as a result of the READI experience. Several counties have participated in economic development projects.

The project also provides a means for working with other agencies and institutions. For example, many school districts have benefited because one of their teachers is a READI instructor. This instructor is able to bring new ideas, materials, and resources into the school as a result of the READI connection. READI benefits, in turn, because the instructors introduce READI courses into the schools. In other partnerships, the Cooperative Extension Service and vocational education programs in small-business management and farm management provide follow-up to the READI classes. Local businesses have sent employees to participate as READI students and as advisory committee members. Finally, READI graduates have often returned to school for credit classes.

Summary

Idaho, like many other states with large rural populations, must come to terms with the increasingly desperate economic and social problems resulting from high levels of unemployment and deindustrialization, lack of mobility, declining educational resources, and technological illiteracy. Computer literacy programs provide a means for dealing with change because they offer resources to break this vicious cycle of poor educational background, high unemployment, and increased social problems. The success of the READI project illustrates that bringing educational opportunity to rural communities can affect both an individual's and a community's future in a positive way.

Mary Emery is the director of the READI project at the University of Idaho, Moscow, Idaho.

Practical skills related to foreign trade are provided to small businesses that may have a product to export.

Educating Small Business for an International Marketplace

Barbara H. Moebius

The increased importance of international markets to both local and national economies and the staggering trade deficit are the impetus for the International Trade Technical Center at Waukesha County Technical Institute in Pewaukee, Wisconsin. This center presents workshops with hands-on practical experience for small and medium-sized businesses in the conducting of international trade; it also develops instructional materials to be used in group and autotutorial settings, and it disseminates these materials around the country.

"Export for America's Future," the theme of World Trade Week, May 1986, reflects the importance of exports to our nation's welfare. There was a time when exporting had a low priority in the United States. The vast size of our domestic markets and the ease with which American goods were sold abroad after World War II allowed us to become complacent. There was little foreign competition.

All of that has changed drastically. According to U.S. Department of Commerce figures, since 1960 our share of world trade has dropped from 18 percent to 15 percent. Today, 70 percent of all U.S goods compete at home and abroad with foreign-made goods. In 1985, the value of manufactured goods exported by the U.S. trailed West German and Japanese exports by sizable margins. As a percentage of gross national product,

U.S. exports declined 20 percent from 1979 to 1983. This rate far exceeded that of any other major industrialized nation. Only 10 percent, or 30,000 out of 300,000, U.S. firms export. Less than 1 percent of those firms do 80 percent of the exporting. The Department of Commerce estimates that 18,000 more firms have exportable products, but ignorance of the opportunity and fear of the unknown are among the major factors preventing them from entering the global marketplace.

Compounding these problems is the fact that the U.S imports far more than it exports. The last time a trade surplus was registered was in 1981. Alarming increases in the trade deficit, from $9 billion in 1982 to $148.5 billion in 1985, alerted the nation that something needed to be done.

Nowhere has this been more obvious than in what has come to be known as the Rust Bowl of the Midwest. Old manufacturing cities with smokestack industries that were once flagships of the region have been hard hit by foreign competition from automobiles to machine tools. Layoffs and plant closings have become common. For every $1 billion in lost exports, 25,000 jobs disappear. Surviving industries and entrepreneurial efforts clearly need workers trained in international trade if they are going to compete in the global marketplace.

Some of the businesses affected by the changing economy are of sufficient size to develop their own international training divisions. Others, however, belong to the small-business category that is responsible for the creation of two-thirds of the new jobs in this country. The health of these small businesses is critical to the national economy, but they are too small to have their own international resource and training facilities. They are not familiar with the complex, nation-specific regulations for exporting, and they quickly become discouraged by the complexities with which their initial efforts are met.

The Associate Degree Program

In 1983, Waukesha County Technical Institute (WCTI), located on the western edge of the greater Milwaukee metropolitan area, began a two-pronged approach to addressing the issues just described. In direct response to requests from area employers and on the basis of a market survey that assessed the level of employment opportunities for graduates, the associate degree in international trade was offered in 1984. Enrollment quickly grew from thirty-eight in 1984 to more than 100 in 1986.

The International Trade Technical Center

In 1985, WCTI began development of a resource and reference center that would contain extensive information on all aspects of international trade. Trained personnel at the center would help area businesses find needed information, and this staff would be available to answer questions over the telephone. The references would include indexes, handbooks, directories, and guides to foreign firms; worldwide marketing, statistical, and media guides; country and regional information; journals, periodicals, and newspapers; government publications and forms; and audiovisual materials.

With a two-year grant from the Fund for the Improvement of Postsecondary Education, the proposed resource and reference center became an actuality. Called the International Trade Technical Center, it works closely with business and industry to determine the type of continuing education and training programs needed for effective participation in the global marketplace, both by companies presently engaged and by those new to exporting. An advisory committee composed of twelve local representatives from small and medium-sized businesses, government, education, transportation, finance, and an export management company guide the selection of programming, target markets, reference materials, and available services. Members also offer suggestions on cooperation and coordination to avoid duplicating other services in the metropolitan Milwaukee area.

The Workshops and Target Audiences. Sources of rudimentary training at the local level on a continuing education basis have been, for the most part, unavailable in the Midwest. Training centers that are already established focus on the needs of executives and other top management personnel in larger firms, and these are mainly located on the East and West Coasts. In contrast, the objectives of the International Trade Technical Center include customized training for owners of small and medium-sized firms whose prosperity depends on extending their markets into other nations. Many of these are managed by self-made entrepreneurs with narrowly focused technical educations or business skills. Many managers lack research skills needed to expand their businesses to include exporting. The first workshop offering, "Developing an Export Program," was targeted for this group.

The center also offers training for skilled technical and clerical employees whose responsibilities have been increased to include some aspect of international trade. In smaller businesses, the employer usually does not provide specialized training. Two highly successful workshops, "Export Documentation and Payment Methods" and "Moving Cargo Internationally," were designed for this group. They focused on providing hands-on practical experience in preparing documents related to the flow of goods and money internationally, and they presented an overview of air and ocean transportation and the shipment of hazardous cargo. A tour of a cargo-loading vessel helped participants see how their products were handled.

A third target group includes food distributors and agribusinesses who need to diversify products and markets. This audience needs to acquire a more comprehensive understanding of the global marketplace. A workshop on "Opportunities in Asia" focused on understanding market potential and special export requirements for this region. Upcoming workshops include "Communicating Internationally" and "How to Find an Overseas Distributor."

Current students in the WCTI associate degree program in international trade also benefit from the workshops through enhanced educational opportunities and interaction with practitioners in the field. For example, a seminar entitled "Trade and Investment Opportunities in Thailand" is being held with no charge to the public; all students, regardless of their financial resources, will be able to take advantage of it. (Normally, workshops cost $50 for a full-day program.)

The potential audience of the workshops has been extended greatly by videotaping each one. Every issue covered in the seminars has been edited and packaged as stand-alone information on the practical aspects of international trade. Any business or continuing education agency may contact WCTI for use of these tapes at the nominal cost of reproduction. They are available from the International Trade Technical Center at Waukesha County Technical Institute in Pewaukee, Wisconsin.

The workshops offered by the center provide information and skills that are directly transferable to the workplace, with virtually no emphasis on theory. Participants bring questions to the workshops that have arisen in their daily work life. They receive immediate, relevant answers from the workshop presenters. This process integrates the information they are learning with the work setting in which it will be used.

Organizations can now let the center know about their specific continuing education training needs, and it will respond with customized training programs. These businesses can use the videotaped materials to conduct in-house training programs for employees who are unable to attend the original workshops.

Other Services. Since public awareness of international trade issues has increased, more programming is being offered by a variety of state and federal agencies, local trade clubs, educational and financial institutions, as well as private consulting firms. As a public service, the center provides dissemination of information to over 6,000 potential users of this type of continuing education, minimizing duplication and increasing awareness and participation in educational opportunities statewide.

A support group for those new to exporting has been organized through the center. This group, cognizant of the difficulties they faced in their earliest efforts toward exporting, is trying to reach the small business with an exportable product that is not aware of the potential market abroad and is not a member of a world trade organization. The U.S.

Department of Commerce, International Trade Division, attempts to do this, but budget and personnel costs have seriously curtailed their efforts. In addition to identifying businesses with exportable products, the support group is developing a fact sheet with answers to the most basic questions asked by someone considering exporting. More important, a resource pool of experienced exporters who are willing to answer questions by telephone on specific topics is developing. The impetus for this group came, not from the center, but from several businesses that had used our services. One key to success for a center such as ours is just this type of responsiveness to what the target market tells the center it needs.

Lessons Learned. Initially, we thought that two- to three-day workshops that exhaustively treated each topic would be the best way to provide continuing education for those already employed. We discovered, however, that it is difficult for employees to be away from their duties at work for more than one day at a time, and we modified our workshop format accordingly.

Similarly, we expected small and medium-sized businesses to utilize the center on a drop-in basis, but we have found they often do not have the time or the staff to spare for research. For preliminary reports, they much prefer to contract with the center to provide the needed information. During the second year of the project, information will be gathered on an ad hoc basis by using students from the associate degree program. In this way, the center will provide a service, the students will gain visibility with area firms, and the firms will obtain the information they need. When federal funding runs out, we hope that these firms will recognize the importance of the center and become a source of financial support for continuation of the service.

Outcomes. Project outcomes include: a growing awareness of the global nature of the nation's economy; development among local small businesses of the necessary skills for export activities, including accessing and utilizing resources of information; and increasing sensitivity to cultural differences affecting business practices in other nations. Students in the associate degree program are gaining the ability to compete in the arena of international trade by developing marketable skills. Through the videotapes and self-paced learning materials, other businesses and postsecondary institutions are improving and extending their educational programs.

The Value of Partnerships

Recognition of the importance of international trade through almost daily articles in the local newspapers has spawned the development of more programs in this area. It is important to establish channels of communication and coordination with such other local undertakings.

Through advisory boards and other less formal means of communication, duplication of effort can be avoided and concentration on quality programming accomplished by educational institutions working together.

Visibility in the business community can be obtained through forums provided by the state Department of Development; various world trade associations; export conferences; and radio, newspaper, and television interviews. An initial mailing list can be obtained from these organizations. They can provide you with much guidance in early stages. They became the project's cheerleaders, spreading the word through their own networks.

Being successful is another way to make the project visible, and it results in other organizations making themselves known to you. Small-business associations, with fertile candidates for those new to exporting, are among groups with whom you should become aligned. In Wisconsin, the Department of Agriculture, Trade, and Consumer Protection can penetrate the agricultural and forestry industries. The local International Trade Division of the U.S. Department of Commerce is an invaluable source of leads and assistance. Cosponsoring workshops with these groups extends networks and allows tapping of valuable expertise.

A needs assessment survey is a vital first step in determining the export training needs of your target market. Membership of the state's various world trade clubs and the exporters listed in the state directory of manufacturers will provide lists of respondents to help ensure that the workshops provide the desired content.

The biggest factor in the success of this type of continuing education program is the commitment of the chief executive officer of the sponsoring institution. The information sources necessary to support the requisite training cost two to three times the usual library acquisitions for program support. It takes a full year to develop recognition, support, and acknowledgement from the state and local agencies who can assist your efforts. Without commitment from the highest levels in the institution, educators will find it difficult to offer and to continue to offer quality programming. The same is true for businesses seeking to establish export markets: The sales or marketing manager cannot do it without the support of the CEO.

The greatest difficulty in undertaking the task of building something from nothing is time. Having carefully planned what needs to be done and then how to go about doing it, project designers often expect things to happen much more quickly than they do. In retrospect, our planning probably did not take into account all of the individuals, departments, and divisions that needed to be coordinated in order to make the plans a reality. Adapting and editing workshop presentations for use as stand-alone modules is a difficult task and extremely time-consuming. Patience and perserverance are qualities needed to ensure success.

The Wisconsin Department of Development, the Small Business Administration, the U.S. Department of Commerce, the Wisconsin Department of Agriculture, Trade, and Consumer Protection, the four world trade associations, various chambers of commerce, the university and university extension system, the vocational, technical, and adult education system, and various independent colleges are now meeting, coordinating, and at times cosponsoring programs. Greater success can be achieved through combined programming and networks than can be accomplished alone. A spirit of cooperation in working together to increase awareness of the global economy, to facilitate exporting, and to develop employment opportunities exists in Wisconsin today.

Barbara H. Moehius is project director of the International Trade Technical Center at the Waukesha County Technical Institute in Pewaukee, Wisconsin. She has lived and studied in Japan and is a consultant for doing business with the Japanese.

Lessons from the case studies offer new considerations and directions for integrating education and work.

Improving Practice: Lessons from the Case Studies

Catherine A. Rolzinski, Ivan Charner

The six case studies presented in this sourcebook provide examples of educational institutions entering new partnerships to respond to problems arising from the changing economy. The projects suggest future possibilities for innovative connections between continuing education and economic concerns. The Education and the Economy Alliance also has implications for the entire range of postsecondary education as well as for business and industry, for community leaders and organizations, and for counselors and planners in related fields.

In Chapter One, we traced the structural changes facing the economy and put forth a framework for examining the resources that comprise the continuing education enterprise—clients, content, modes of delivery, and sources. In this chapter, we will take a second look at these resources and determine what they can mean for integrating education and work when the framework is applied to actual practice.

Lessons drawn from the case studies are in some ways specific to each project, but there are also important themes that transcend the separate projects. These more generic themes are shared not only by the six projects presented in this volume but also by all twenty-five of the projects in the alliance. The themes introduce another perspective for practitioners to use in conceptualizing or planning a collaborative effort between education and new partners, such as business, unions, the community, or a new group of adult learners.

We will use the case studies themselves to explore the components of productive partnerships and emphasize the issues of time and community-based perceptions, of position and authority, and of flexibility. We will also look at what the case studies tell us about the meaning and functioning of community, about community leaders and organizations, and about the ramifications of position. Finally, we identify new directions for integrating education and work on behalf of the adult learner.

Productive Partnerships

Establishing new partnerships was a strategy selected by all twenty-five projects in the alliance to respond to problems resulting from changes in the economy. The experience of forming partnerships between educational institutions and businesses, unions, government agencies, and community groups made the issues of the partners' different perceptions and perspectives a common refrain in the project stories. Intangible and unforeseen conflicts involving questions of tradition, orientation, points of view, culture, responsibility, attitudes, and mission were identified as some of the most serious, complex, and sometimes insurmountable problems, especially in the planning and early implementation stages. Time to deal with these issues was an ongoing need.

Time and Perceptions. A tremendous amount of time and care must be taken for all of the partners involved to get to know one another. This process requires from each partner a willingness to increase self-awareness and to gain valuable new insights into idiosyncratic ways of perceiving roles and missions. Only when this process is recognized from the beginning as a continual and invaluable priority will new partnerships have the expanded perspective needed to accomplish their goals.

The importance of giving time and attention to perceiving and confronting assumptions is supported by the case studies. In Chapter Four, for example, Lamdin and Hassan ascribe the "agonizingly slow first six months" of the Business Development and Training Center to just such underlying assumptions: "Public relations efforts were inadequate, and, even among those who had heard of it, the BDTC was viewed as an unknown quantity with an imperfectly understood mission." For this project, the process of relinquishing predetermined perceptions was definitely a two-way street; as the authors conclude, "This new educational services model, created in the high-minded naïveté of the academic world, has had to make a myriad of adjustments to the reality of corporate America."

In Chapter Five, Derber describes similar discoveries:

> We found it essential to develop close and relaxed working relations with influential union officials before we embarked

on the joint design of educational programs for their members. The development of these relationships requires far more time and patience than we had anticipated—often more than a year simply to establish the requisite trust.

Substantial time is required as well for any outsider to get the "lay of the land" both within the union and the plant and in the industrial environment in general.

And in Chapter Seven, Moebius states:

The greatest difficulty in undertaking the task of building something from nothing is time. Having carefully planned what needs to be done and then how to go about doing it, project designers often expect things to happen much more quickly than they do. In retrospect, our planning probably did not take into account all of the individuals, departments, and divisions that needed to be coordinated in order to make the plans a reality.

These excerpts from the case studies exemplify what can be learned from candidly taking stock.

One problem of new partnerships between education and business is that, even with the best of intentions, it is difficult for each party to realize and overcome stereotypes about the values and operating principles of the other, as Skinner, Siefer, and Shovers point out in Chapter Two: "Despite enthusiasm about expected benefits and mutual respect, educators and employers are most likely to abandon partnerships of this type . . . because of differences in customary approaches to work." Each organization has its own distinct pattern of behavior. In entering a partnership, each organization faces challenges to its long-standing traditions and accepted behavior. Power and decision-making authority are also threatened as the prospective partners struggle over how to share their new roles and responsibilities.

Position and Authority. The position within the overall structure of the project director, as well as his or her relationship to visible authority and the power to sanction, were crucial to the success of the projects. In addition, the placement of the project within the most appropriate organizational unit in the partner organization was very important. Perceptions of legitimacy depended upon positioning, and this was often a critical factor in the transition from the project being viewed as marginal to its full acceptance by the partner organizations. Langer makes this clear in Chapter Three.

The numerous and timely decisions necessary for the project's success demanded top administrative support. MATC's dean of the Technical and Industrial Division, as well as the executive dean, chief executive officer, and the board of directors were all committed to providing the support and flexibility required by the project. The top-level assistance was needed to overcome the confusion of the bureaucratic maze, state contract laws, the budget process, and to meet important timetables and negotiate industrial partnerships.

In Chapter Six, the issues of positioning and authority are resolved through community "ownership" of the project:

The READI project has been developed on the assumption that local communities or county committees will take responsibility for running the project on the local level. University extension or continuing education programs share responsibility by providing additional expertise, help with networking, and access to a support person. This arrangement of shared responsibility and risk results in a program with local ownership and control but with expanded resources.

Flexibility. By recognizing the importance of the factors related to perceptions, time, and positioning, partners ensure flexibility in their collaborative education and work programs. One primary reason for the importance of such flexibility is illustrated in Chapter Two:

The structure of relationships between educators and the workplace must be flexible enough to survive the frequent changes that occur in the workplace. . . . In a little more than two years, the Honeywell liaison person with ASU changed three times. In addition, many of the key members of the partnership changed their job positions and locations within the company several times when major staff reorganizations occurred.

The closer we look at partnership arrangements, the more we see this need for flexibility. The early planning relationship between potential partners is a conceptual stage, and, as the concept is translated to action, the priorities and style of the partners will merge. The sharing of information, personnel, responsibility, and programming produces a halting movement forward as formal policies and procedures and informal methods of implementation are changed. Only partners who are open and flexible and who can agree to go "back to the drawing board" as often as is necessary will bring conceptual ideas to functioning fruition. As the partners move toward their common goal, however, a spirit of collegiality and shared ownership evolves.

The case studies validate the conclusion that the integration of education and work is not easy, nor is there any one prescriptive guide that provides all of the answers to any particular situation. Partnerships between education and businesses, unions, government agencies, and community groups are not yet a natural condition in this society. Many linkages arise in reaction to problems from changing economic forces, and this reactive condition compounds the complexity of achieving productive partnerships.

The usual planning approach in such new partnerships begins with identifying the economic problem to be addressed. Then, strategies are developed that focus on the elements of clients, content, modes of delivery, and sources. Drawing from the alliance experience, however, the considerations deemed to be more complex in the planning stages are those relating to perceptions, time, position, authority, and flexibility.

The following questions can help guide the planning process toward establishing more productive partnership programs:

1. What are the benefits and risks for each institution or organization in the partnership?

2. Where does decision-making authority for the project sit among the leaders of each postsecondary institution, business, union, community group, or government agency?

3. What are the powers, resources, and perceptions that accompany the project placement?

4. What are the perceptions and stereotypes held by each group in the partnership about the nature, style, mission, and content—the "culture"—of the other partners?

5. How much serious time and attention are the partners willing to give to the more subtle and unforeseen problems that relate to the cultural differences between them?

6. How can flexibility be built into the partnership arrangement?

Education and Community Economic Development

Key elements for integrating education and work have to do with the perceptions and involvement of the community to be affected by the economic development endeavor. The notion of community and all of its ramifications has been central to the success of most of the projects in the alliance.

Community. The term "community economic development" refers to planning and implementing programs to improve the economic well-being of people within their social context. Getting to know a community or doing a needs assessment of a community is considered standard practice in the process of designing economic development programs and strategies. But just what is a "community"?

For our purposes, a community is defined as a group of people who perceive things in a common way or have interests, work, tastes, ownership, or participation in common. Currently, at least three distinctly different kinds of communities have a need to work together—education, business, and adult learners.

Frequent usage of a word like "community" can inure new partners to its meaning; without intending to do so, they will interpret other people's situations based simply on their own sense of community. With different perceptions coming from the education, business, and adult-learner communities, tremendous barriers can be created.

Knowing how to dress, talk, and socialize appropriately comprises part of the "culture" of a community. All of these known elements provide community members with a certain degree of security that can be easily shaken when faced with the unfamiliar. For educators to collaborate successfully in economic development endeavors, they need to look beyond the demographics and relinquish their own sense of security in order to try to experience people's circumstances within their different communities. This process is essential to building trust and provides the groundwork for effective community economic development.

One of the most important notions of community boils down to interdependence. Despite opposing forces, Americans seek a sense of community and have difficulty facing a change in life-style. In the Northwest, for instance, the majority of workers in the timber industry have stayed on long after their jobs have ended. Unemployed and displaced workers are often proud people who have gained a tremendous amount of knowledge and skills that seem to have no current value. These adults may confront the prospect of education as a means to a new way of life, but for many of them the prospect of further education is more remote than a foreign country.

Community Leaders and Organizations. Existing community-based organizations and the "right" community leaders can serve as bridges between communities of people in need of improved economic opportunities and the continuing educators who want to help. Most community-based organizations are involved in some kind of community education with such common characteristics as the following:

- Serving the community via a grass-roots approach
- Relying on forms of learning not identified with traditional postsecondary education
- Relating more to function than form in education and training programs
- Practicing a democratic process in local community improvement.

Many community-based leaders have a bias against educational institutions, and traditional educators often have their own biased views of community-based educators and organizations. Community leaders often feel that educational institutions do not recognize and appreciate their distinctiveness and cannot develop and deliver educational programs appropriate to their particular community needs. On the other hand, traditional educators rarely have had the training or the organizational support to allow them to experience community-based education. Since each group comes from such disparate backgrounds and collaborative attempts on both sides have often been limited and superficial, mutual suspicion can prevail. The case study of the READI project (Chapter Six) offers a clear example of acknowledging the special characteristics of each community:

> Since rural areas are known for the way they cherish traditional values, the committee must mediate between the need for constancy within the community and the press for change. For each community, as with each individual, this balance is unique. What is acceptable in one area may not work in another. The READI approach provides for flexible schedules and program design, allowing classes to differ from community to community. The local committee monitors the success of the courses based on local criteria.

When such an advisory committee is formed, the important question to guide the selection of members is, "What parts of the community, higher education, and business need to be represented?" This lesson is clearly demonstrated in Chapter Three's case study:

> A steering committee was appointed to guide development of the project. Committee members included leaders in automation who represented the industries to be served by graduates and retrained employees. Representatives of labor unions, professional associations, high schools, and universities also served on the committee.
>
> Significant factors in the project's success were the use of community leaders and the infrastructure of the committee itself.

Integrating Education and Work on Behalf of the Adult Learner

Who are the prospective learners in education and work ventures? First, most of these potential new students are adults. Today, many of these adults are in their thirties, forties, or fifties and have been working in, and identifying with, a particular kind of industry for most of their lives.

During the three years of the alliance's existence, the twenty-five project directors came together three times a year to share experiences and to identify emerging themes that might highlight policy implications or new directions for integrating education and work. Three of the most prominent themes that surfaced were learner-centered education, economic literacy, and liberal education.

Learner-Centered Education. Adult learners are mature and experienced; they are looking for educational programs that are responsive to their employment needs and to their responsibilities as citizens. With the backgrounds that these new students bring to adult, continuing, and extension education, they tend to respond to a different kind of pedagogy than that of traditional postsecondary institutions. Appropriate pedagogy includes a more active and participatory kind of learning; this is not the style employed by the majority of faculty.

Improved educational opportunities are needed that focus directly on the conditions and situations relevant to and identifiable by the adult worker. New programs to integrate education and work ought to convey the centrality of the learner in the educational process through the design and delivery of content, instruction, and skill development that empower the learner. As Emery points out in Chapter Six:

> The first principle is that adults learn best by doing, particularly with activities that have a direct application to some part of their lives. For hands-on activities to be successful, however, the instruction must go beyond drill and practice and must involve the students in the discovery of knowledge. In short, neither content nor method in the READI curriculum represents a technical approach to providing computer literacy; rather, READI approaches computer literacy from a problem-solving focus with an emphasis on group interaction.

Economic Literacy. As the Boston College experience (Chapter Five) suggests:

> Workers desperately need access to many kinds of knowledge currently reserved for management: knowledge about their own industry and the nature of the new global production and market, information about national and regional economic trends, understanding of new technological developments and the kinds of skills likely to be in demand both in their own and in other industries, and education for social and economic planning and development. This kind of "economic literacy," a precondition for worker self-management and for a proactive labor movement, is not a significant part of any of the prevailing models of labor education.

The need for economic literacy translates to the need for increasing sophistication regarding the role of the economy among the American populace. Since workers now face job retraining and job change as a matter of course in their work lives, they need to understand how the job market is affected by various trends in order to be effective in their life and work planning. Not only individual workers but also entire communities find their futures in jeopardy as a result of economic changes. Community members require information and the skills to use that information to plan successfully for their future.

Possible components of economic literacy are:

- Basic economic terminology, such as that used in the media and in policy statements to describe economic changes
- Basic economic data, particularly those used to convey to the public what is happening in the economy
- Information on specific industries that touch the clients' lives most directly
- Occupational/job-related skills, particularly those necessary to function in the changing workplace
- Knowledge and skills necessary for the new level of community participation necessary in economic planning and development decisions
- Knowledge necessary to understand the global economy and how it affects the local, regional, and national economies
- Some basic knowledge of consumer economics.

The American economy has always been in transition, but in the last several decades these changes have taken place at a much faster rate. The need for informed participation regarding the economy and how it relates to an individual's life makes economic literacy more critical than ever before. A proactive teaching strategy enables adult workers to get information and to make critical decisions about the economy as it affects a particular workplace, a job search, or larger economic developments in the country and the world.

One method of teaching and learning economic literacy that was used in several alliance projects was that of participatory research. Participatory research is an integrated approach that combines research, education, and action around an issue or issues deemed important for a community, workplace group, or other collectivity. Central to this approach is the conviction that residents or members of these groups can learn to define their issues, do most of their own research, educate each other, and participate in collective activities to solve their problems.

Two rural community economic development projects, in particular, are involving their communities in this way. In the Southeast, the Highlander Research and Education Center in New Market, Tennessee, is sponsoring the Highlander Economics Education Project. This project operates a participatory research and education program that enables residents of rural Appalachian communities to deal more effectively with the impact of the changing economy on their lives. The project develops models of cooperation as local community colleges and grass-roots community groups work together to meet community and individual needs resulting from current economic change. It also develops an economics curriculum that provides the rural residents with the educational base for dealing with ongoing economic change.

The success of the READI project in Idaho is based on the careful way that the project staff worked with an advisory group on a county-by-county basis and trained local resource people to teach the classes. With limited resources, community groups learned how to utilize educational strategies relating to their rural isolation and ways to identify how technology could spur economic development.

When education and community groups work together and design an educational process to provide the tools to identify and analyze the varied resources that the community has, a new learning constituency is established. This permits communities to look at how larger economic forces affect them, to identify the possible options for revitalizing the local economy, to decide on the most desirable approaches, and to develop the feasible and best strategies.

Liberal Education. The impetus for educators to get involved with economic problems is usually an immediate need arising from rapid changes in labor market conditions. This urgency encourages employers, faculty, and advisers to think initially only about the short term. But these educational partnerships with business could offer the learners a whole new kind of liberal education. It is probably useful to distinguish between the "liberal arts," traditionally defined as a substantive body of knowledge that defines and shapes culture, society, and ideas, and "liberal education," in this sense, an education or learning experience liberating one personally and providing the skills and knowledge to be more effective, self-confident, competent, and self-directed.

The valued characteristics of a liberal education include:
- Critical and analytical skill development
- Formation of abstract concepts
- Comparative analysis of abstractions
- Learning to learn
- Objectivity.

While abstract discussions may emphasize differences between vocational and academic education, the case studies in this sourcebook reveal that, in practice, both endeavors seek to transmit the same underlying skills. Skinner, Siefer, and Shovers highlight this point in Chapter Two:

> The Language Working training program helped to develop the kind of worker that industry wants and liberal

education promotes: an individual trained to communicate effectively, think critically, make decisions, and work as part of a team. The program emphasized the dynamic language skills required to cope with the changing nature of today's work environments. Worker-students learned strategies for adapting to change and for acquiring and imparting new knowledge.

Summary

As continuing educators give more emphasis to problems arising from the changing economy, they are faced with the issues of forming partnerships (or some type of new collaborative arrangement) with business, organized labor, government, and community groups. The case studies presented in this volume and the lessons derived from them can be utilized as a springboard for creative planning of new partnerships that integrate education and work while realizing the unique local issues of each community.

Effective continuing education providers should use these linkages and partnerships to help adult learners develop the knowledge and skills necessary to *continue* to learn for their changing roles in the workplace and the community. Integrating education and work, then, becomes a powerful ongoing strategy for all organizations involved and for adult learners taking charge of their lives, careers, and community development.

Catherine A. Rolzinski is a consultant in the areas of education and economic development based in Washington, D.C.

Ivan Charner is director of research and development at the National Institute for Work and Learning in Washington, D.C.

Questions and issues are raised for the future of integrating education and work.

Critical Questions and Issues for Integrating Education and Work

Ivan Charner, Catherine A. Rolzinski

Is the integration of education and work merely a passing fad, or does it represent a fundamental shift for the role of continuing education? The changes anticipated for the economy will continue to apply pressure on education to become more involved in economic, community, and human resource development, suggesting that a fundamental shift in the relationship between continuing education and work is at hand. In this concluding chapter, we present a set of critical questions and issues for continuing education. These questions provide a perspective for looking at the future integration of education and work. The framework presented in Chapter One is used to organize the questions and issues.

Clients

Will the future parallel the present with regard to clients? Can adult and continuing education effectively serve the needs of individual adult learners while increasingly trying to respond to the wants and desires of businesses, unions, and community organizations? It seems safe to conclude that declining enrollments of traditional-age students combined with budget constraints due to tax and fiscal policies will require the continuing education enterprise to seek new clients. These new clients will not only include new groups of adult workers (such as women, older workers, immigrants, retirees, union members, and rural adults) but also organizations, such as businesses, community groups, and unions. The first question for continuing educators, then, is: How can more programs like those described in this volume be developed to attract new clients to the continuing education system?

A second question follows naturally from the first: How can continuing educators identify the education and training needs of these diverse client groups? If continuing education providers look to businesses and other organizations as their primary client groups, how will this affect services to individual adult workers? Are the goals and needs of these client groups in conflict, or can both be served through one system? Are the concepts of "economic literacy" and "liberal education" in conflict, or can they go hand in hand to the betterment of all? Finally, will the notion of "who can pay" determine who will be served by the continuing education system? Or can a balance be reached so that all of those in need of continuing education and training programs can be served?

Content

As demographics, economics, and technology continue to change, what are the skills, information, knowledge, and attitudes that adults and organizations will need? How can the content of continuing education and training be responsive to the shifts that are anticipated? The case studies presented in this volume represent a growing number of postsecondary programs that are providing a wide range of content in education and training. Basic skills and remedial courses are being offered by corporations in increasing numbers. Adult basic education and literacy programs are also on the rise among community organizations. At the same time, two- and four-year colleges are offering basic skills programs to adults. Will these programs, operating at the workplace, in the community, and in educational institutions, have to grow as more adults are found to have inadequate basic skills preparation to meet the challenges of the future?

Continuing education programs in job skills (vocational, retraining, and upgrading) have also been on the upswing. As new technologies have been developed and as sectors of the labor force have been affected by economic shifts, the need for new skills has been created. Continuing education programs offered by diverse sources have been responding to this need. How can continuing educators better anticipate these changes throughout the remainder of this century and well into the next? If the nation's businesses and human resources are to keep pace with technological shifts and economic changes, will more programs for retraining, upgrading, international trade, and skill development have to be made available to broader populations of businesses and adult workers?

As new technologies are developing and as sectors in the labor force are changing, it is predicted that managers and professionals will need new knowledge in diverse areas ranging from specific skills, to entrepreneurship, to human resource planning. What will be the appropriate role for continuing education in professional skill upgrading to keep pace with technological and economic shifts and in management skill development to be responsive to the changing nature of the workplace and the adult worker? The roles and responsibilities of business, education, government, and individuals in the changing work environment have yet to be worked out.

Outreach, counseling, and information services are being made available to various client groups through continuing education programs. As the economy continues to change, will there be a need for increasing such services, and, if so, is the continuing education enterprise the most appropriate institutional base for providing personal and family counseling? Should continuing education be the source of information on the structure and dynamics of the local labor market; education and training opportunities; new technologies; human resource planning and development; projected supply-demand imbalances in human resources; and changes in economic structures? How can educational institutions work with other organizations to provide the support services that may be needed in the future?

A few other questions related to the content of continuing education and training should be considered in response to changing realities. First, as the population ages and a larger proportion faces retirement, what role will continuing education play in offering programs and services to this segment of the population? Clearly, some persons will need to be trained or retrained in order to continue to earn a living (or to supplement retirement income). Others will need vocational or avocational programs as they are faced with more free time. Are approaches that integrate these new learners with students of other age groups better, or does this population require its own set of programs?

Second, the role of general/liberal/humanistic education in a changing economy needs to be examined. Should continuing educators take the lead in refocusing the nation's attention on the importance of this category of education in the years ahead? Should programs on humanities and business, liberal arts and technology, critical thinking, and so on, be developed as necessary alternatives to existing approaches to vocational training? What is the role of liberal and general education in "education for work" programs? How can work-, job-, and career-oriented programs be used as vehicles for teaching critical thinking, abstract reasoning, and learning-to-learn skills commonly transmitted through liberal arts and humanities programs? What should the balance be between liberal arts and the humanities as a vehicle for preparation for work, on the one hand, and education for work as a vehicle for transmitting general and liberal arts skills and knowledge on the other?

Third, what is the appropriate role for continuing education to play in relationship to economic literacy and to community-level planning and facilitation of economic development? Should continuing education institutions take the lead in developing strategies in these areas, or should they be participants in a process initiated by other organizations?

Finally, as new management approaches call for increased worker participation in decisions, is it necessary for programs to be offered to adult workers that provide them with critical-thinking skills appropriate to these new roles? Also, as individuals are faced with increasing job and career changes, will they need more programs that provide skills and opportunities for decision making based on reliable information? Will such programs be in direct conflict with services to meet the needs of businesses and corporations?

Modes of Delivery

Different modes have long been used to deliver continuing education and training to adults. As changes in the economy affect postsecondary education, will increased reliance on alternative methods be necessary? In addition to the traditional learning approaches of lectures and small-group lecture-discussions, other approaches should be explored.

Can new approaches to scheduling, course structure, timing, and method of instruction offer continuing education and training opportunities to larger numbers of different clients? Use of new technologies such as teletext, teleconferencing, interactive video, and computers can also offer learning approaches to wide audiences. How can education and training institutions be more flexible in their delivery of programs to learners? Experiments and demonstrations that use alternative modes of delivery should be tried. Unless the traditional providers of continuing education and training are willing to offer alternatives to the standard approaches, they may lose out to other providers of postsecondary education who are willing and able to offer almost any course or program at almost any time, almost anywhere. Up to $40 billion that is currently spent by corporations for training is at stake. As individuals and organizations respond to changes in technology and in the economy, they will want educational delivery systems that help them to move quickly and efficiently.

Sources

Sources of continuing education and training are abundant and diverse. As the labor market continues to change in response to demographic and economic shifts, these sources of education and training should become more responsive. Will new programs be needed as more workers are displaced or as more move into the information and service sectors of the labor force? Will continuing educators need to look closely at the other sources of education and training to fill gaps in programs, adults served, and services offered? How can the more traditional providers of continuing education programs recognize the magnitude and importance of the "shadow" education system and develop partnerships to reduce overlap, redundancy, and competition in an attempt to serve better both employees and employers?

Are new sources of education and training needed in the near future, or can better use be made of existing sources to respond to the changing economic and social realities facing the nation in the next quarter century?

Summary

A number of critical questions and issues concerning the clients, content, delivery, and sources of the continuing education enterprise have been raised. They bring into focus the dramatic changes in the continuing education system that may result from changes in the direction and pace of the economy. They also make clear the need for integrating education and work as an effective way of responding to these changes.

The discussion in Chapter Eight of the factors central to developing productive partnerships offers a set of new considerations and directions for integrating education and work. Policy makers and practitioners are encouraged to examine these alternatives in light of the questions and issues raised above. For continuing education to be responsive to the needs of new client groups, it must look beyond its traditional role toward its emerging role in economic, community, and human resource development. It must be more proactive in its responses to the diverse needs of a diverse society. The continuing education system cannot work alone; it needs to work in partnership with businesses, unions, government, and community organizations. Nor can the continuing education system offer limited options; it must offer a comprehensive set of services delivered in a variety of ways to individuals and organizations. And continuing educators cannot only be concerned with education; they need to be equally concerned with learning—learning that empowers individuals and organizations not only to respond to but also to anticipate the changes they will be facing in the future. Continuing educators must recognize that the integrating of education and work is not a passing fad. Rather, it is a strategy that offers exciting opportunities for a challenging future.

Ivan Charner is director of research and development at the National Institute for Work and Learning in Washington, D.C.

Catherine A. Rolzinski is a consultant in the areas of education and economic development based in Washington, D.C.

APPENDIX
List of Projects of the FIPSE Education and the Economy Alliance

Applied Basic Skills: Education for Work
Robert Lee
Jobs for Youth, Inc.
Chicago, Ill.

Cascade Business Development Center: A Small Business Incubator
Samuel Brooks
Portland Community College
Portland, Oreg.

Educational Bridges to Options in High-Technology Employment
Celia Marshak
San Diego State University
San Diego, Calif.

Educational Maintenance Organization
Maxine Ballen Hassan
Business Development and Training Center
Malverne, Pa.

The Employment Transition Program
Jeanne Prial Gordus
University of Michigan
Ann Arbor, Mich.

English-Language Training for the Workplace
Elizabeth Skinner
Arizona State University
Tempe, Ariz.

Evaluating Noncollegiate-Sponsored Instruction
Timothy Donovan
Community Colleges of Vermont
Winooski, Vt.

The Experienced Workers Retraining Program
Michael Maguire
St. Louis Community College-Forest Park
St. Louis, Mo.

The Foresight Program: Education for Career Management in a Changing Economy
   William Charland
   University of Denver
   Denver, Colo.

Fulfillment of the Liberal Arts Mission Through Education and Research for Area Economic Recovery
   John Agria
   Thiel College
   Greenville, Pa.

Graduate Professional Education for Information Specialists in an Electronic Age
   Richard Budd
   Rutgers University
   New Brunswick, N.J.

Highlander Economics Education Project
   John Gaventa
   Highlander Research and Education Center
   New Market, Tenn.

Intensive In-Plant Technician Training Project
   Stacey Ayers
   Rio Salado Community College
   Phoenix, Ariz.

The International Trade Technical Center
   Barbara Moebius
   Waukesha County Technical Institute
   Pewaukee, Wis.

New Hampshire Industrial Consortia Project
   Eric Brown
   New Hampshire College and University Council
   Manchester, N.H.
   and
   William Andrews
   Monadnock Training Council
   Milford, N.H.

PIC/Higher Education Collaboration Project
   Robert Knight
   National Association of Private Industry Councils
   Washington, D.C.

Postsecondary Adult Literacy Education Project
 John David
 West Virginia Institute of Technology
 Montgomery, W.Va.

Postsecondary Education for a Changing Economy: Resource Agent for Policies and Practices
 Ivan Charner
 National Institute for Work and Learning
 Washington, D.C.

Preparing for High-Technology Careers in Computer-Integrated Manufacturing
 Victor Langer
 Milwaukee Area Technical College
 Milwaukee, Wis.

Public Investment in Higher Education: A Program for New England Legislators
 Melvin Bernstein
 New England Board of Higher Education
 Boston, Mass.

READI: Rural Education/Adult Development in Idaho
 Mary Emery
 University of Idaho
 Moscow, Idaho

School for New Learning Graduate Program
 David Justice
 De Paul University
 Chicago, Ill.

TECPLAY: Technical Education and Career Planning for the Lives of Adults and Youths
 Ann Baker
 Charleston Higher Education Consortium
 Charleston, S.C.

Upper Division BSN for Working RNs
 Michael Petrides
 The College of Staten Island
 Staten Island, N.Y.

Worker Education for the 1980s
 Charles Derber
 Boston College
 Chestnut Hill, Mass.

Index

A

Accreditation Board for Engineering Technology (ABET), 33
Adult learners, education-work integration for, 81-85
AFL-CIO, and worker education, 49-57
Agria, J., 94
Allen-Bradley, and computer-integrated manufacturing, 33
American Banking Institute, 13
American Federation of Teachers (AFT), and worker education, 49, 54
American Management Institute, 13
Andrews, W., 94
Applied Basic Skills: Education for Work, 93
Arizona State University (ASU): Language Working project of, 17-25, 78, 84-85; projects at, 93, 94
ASEA, and computer-integrated manufacturing, 33
Automated manufacturing lab (AML), and computer-integrated manufacturing, 31
Ayers, S., 94

B

Baker, A., 95
Bandura, A., 12, 15
Bernstein, M., 95
Boston, worker education in, 54
Boston College: Social Economy and Social Justice Program of, 49-50; worker education by, 49-57, 82, 94
Bridgeport, and computer-integrated manufacturing, 33
Brooks, S., 93
Brown, E., 94
Budd, R., 94
Business, small, in international trade, 67-73
Business After Hours, 43
Business Development and Training Center (BDTC): analysis of, 39-47, 93; background on, 37-40; career and academic counseling by, 44; and executive seminars, 45; implications of, 47; lessons from, 46; MBA program at, 41-42; and networking, 44-45; newspaper of, 44-45, 46; partnership in, 76; private sector involvement in, 45-46; profile of, 40-45; programs, of, 42-44; and special interest groups, 43-44

C

California, project in, 93
Career Connections Job Service, 39, 45
Carnegie-Mellon University, and computer literacy, 28
Cascade Business Development Center: A Small Business Incubator, 93
Charland, W., 94
Charleston Higher Education Consortium, project at, 95
Charner, I., 2, 3, 5, 15, 75, 85, 87, 92, 95
CIMLING, and computer-integrated manufacturing, 33
Clients: for education-work integration, 10-11; issues of, 87-88
College-Level Examination Program (CLEP), 44
Colorado, project in, 94
Community economic development, 79-81
Compact for Lifelong Educational Opportunities (CLEO), and educational maintenance organization, 39-40, 44, 45
Computer-aided design (CAD): and computer-integrated manufacturing, 27, 29, 31, 32, 35; growth of, 9
Computer-aided manufacturing (CAM): and computer-integrated manufacturing, 31; growth of, 9
Computer education: analysis of, 59-65; approach to, 60-63; availabil-

97

Computer education *(continued)*
ity of, 63-64; lessons from, 78, 81, 82, 84; need for, 59-60; and partnership development, 65; principles of, 61-62; summary on, 65; teacher preparation for, 63

Computer-integrated manufacturing (CIM) education center: analysis of, 27-37; background on, 27-28; and cost-effective workstations, 35; faculty training and selection for, 32; lessons from, 77-78; and performance standards, 33-34; profile of, 29-31; quality elements in, 35-36; and retraining, 34-35; steering committee for, 32; success of, 31-36; and supertech needs, 28; support for, 31-32; technology in, 29-30; and technology leadership, 31, 32-33

Computervision, 33, 35

Content: for education-work integration, 11; issues of, 88-90

Continuing education: clients of, 10-11, 87-88; content of, 11, 88-90; delivery modes for, 11-13, 90; and industrial retraining, 34-35; issues in, 87-92; mandate of, 5; reactive and proactive responses of, 6; sources of, 13-14, 90-91; summary on, 91

Cooperative Extension Service, and computer education, 59, 65

Corporate park, education services in, 39-47

D

David, J., 95

Delaware County Community Center, corporate center training by, 42-43

Delivery modes: for education-work integration, 11-13; issues of, 90

Demographic shifts, 6-7

Denver, University of, project at, 94

De Paul University, project at, 95

Department of Agriculture, Trade, and Consumer Protection (Wisconsin), 72, 73

Department of Development (Wisconsin), 72, 73

Derber, C., 2, 49, 57, 76-77, 96

Developing nations, growth of, 8

Digital Equipment Corporation, and computer-integrated manufacturing, 33

DISCOVER, 44

District of Columbia, projects in, 94, 95

Donovan, T., 93

E

Economic development, community, 79-81

Economic literacy: academic-labor partnerships for, 49-57; for adult learners, 82-84

Economy: changing, 5-15; shifts in, 7-8; structural changes in, 6-10

Education: corporate spending on, 1; learner-centered, 82

Education and the Economy Alliance, 1, 75, 93-96

Education-work integration: for adult learners, 81-85; analysis of, 5-15; background on, 5-6, 75-76; clients for, 10-11, 87-88; and community economic development, 79-81; and computer education, 59-65; in computer-integrated manufacturing education center, 27-37; content for, 11, 88-90; in corporate park, 39-47; delivery modes for, 11-13, 90; and economic shifts, 7-8; implications for, 47; improving practice in, 75-85; and international trade, 67-73; issues in, 87-92; in language project, 17-25; partnerships in, 76-79; quality elements for, 35-36; and social and demographic shifts, 6-7; sources of, 13-14, 90-91; strategies for, 10-14; and structural changes, 6-10; summary on, 14-15, 85, 91; and technological shifts, 8-10; in worker education, 49-57

Educational Bridges to Options in High-Technology Employment, 93

Educational Maintenance Organization (EMO), in corporate park, 39-47, 93

Emery, M., 2, 59, 65, 82, 95

Employment Transition Program, 93

Enerpac, and computer-integrated manufacturing, 33

English-Language Training for the Workplace, 17-25, 93
Evaluating Noncollegiate-Sponsored Instruction, 93
Executive Roundtable, 43
Experienced Workers Retraining Program, 93

F

Fall River, Massachusetts, worker education in, 52-53
Flexible manufacturing cell (FMC), and computer-integrated manufacturing, 27, 31, 33
Foresight Program: Education for Career Management in a Changing Economy, 94
Fulfillment of the Liberal Arts Mission Through Education and Research for Area Economic Recovery, 94
Fund for the Improvement of Postsecondary Education (FIPSE), 1, 29, 33, 40, 49, 56, 59, 69, 93-96

G

Gaventa, J., 94
General Dynamics, Fore River Shipyard of, 53-54
General Electric (GE), and corporate center training, 42-43
General Motors (GM), and worker education, 56
Germany, Federal Republic of: exports from, 67; worker planning in, 50
Gordus, J. P., 93
Graduate Professional Education for Information Specialists in an Electronic Age, 94
Great Valley Corporate Center, and educational maintenance organization, 39-47

H

Hassan, M. B., 2, 39, 47, 76, 93
High-Technology Group, 43
Higher education, as source of education-work integration, 13
Highlander Research and Education Center, Highlander Economics Education Project of, 83-84, 94

Honeywell, Language Working project of, 17-25, 78, 84-85
Hull, D., 28, 36
Human Resource Center, 56
Human resources, collaborative management of, 9-10
Human Resources Managers, 43
Hyman, H., 12, 15

I

Idaho, University of, and computer education, 59-65, 84, 95
Illinois, projects in, 93, 95
Industrial sector, decline of, 7
Instruction, delivery of, 11-13
Intensive In-Plant Technician Training Project, 94
International Ladies' Garment Workers' Union (ILGWU), and worker education, 49, 52-53
International trade: growth of, 8; and number of exports, 67-68
International trade education: analysis of, 67-73; associate degree program in, 68; background on, 67-68; lessons from, 71; outcomes of, 71; and partnerships, 71-73; profile of, 68-71; services in, 70-71; workshops and target audiences for, 69-70
International Trade Technical Center, work of, 67-73, 94
International Union of Maritime and Shipbuilding Workers of America (IUMSWA), and worker education, 49, 53-54
Investment Club, 43

J

James, C. F., 36
Japan: exports from, 67; worker planning in, 50
Jobs, creation and elimination of, 9
Jobs for Youth, 93
Justice, D., 95

K

Kearney-Trecker, and computer-integrated manufacturing, 33
Knight, R., 94

L

Labor education, partnerships for economic literacy in, 49-57
Labor force, women and minorities in, 7, 8
Lamdin, L., 2, 39, 47, 76
Langer, V., 2, 27, 34, 36, 37, 77-78, 95
Language Working: analysis of, 17-25, 93; background on, 17-18; benefits reciprocal in, 19-21; curriculum development for, 19; educator's view of, 20-21; effective working relationship in, 22-24; industry view of, 19-20; lessons from, 78, 84-85; and liberal education, 24-25; needs assessment for, 18-19; pilot program for, 19; profile of, 18-19; skills and knowledge complementary in, 21-22
Lee, R., 93
Liberal education: and adult learners, 84-85; issues of, 89-90; and language training, 24-25

M

Maguire, M., 93
Marshak, C., 93
Massachusetts: projects in, 95, 96; worker education in, 49-57, 96
MBA program, of educational maintenance organization, 41-42
Mead, G., 12, 15
Merton, R., 12, 15
Michigan, University of, project at, 93
Milwaukee Area Technical College (MATC), computer-integrated manufacturing education center of, 27-37, 77-78, 95
Minority workers: English-language training for, 17-25; in labor force, 7
Missouri, project in, 93
MIT Enterprise Forum, 44, 45
Moebius, B. H., 3, 67, 73, 77, 94
Monadnock Training Council, project at, 94

N

National Association of Investment Clubs, 43

National Association of Private Industry Councils, 94
National Computer Graphics Association, 31
National Institute for Work and Learning, 95
New England Board of Higher Education, project at, 95
New Hampshire College and University Council, project at, 94
New Hampshire Industrial Consortia Project, 94
New Jersey, project in, 94
New York, project in, 95
Numeridex, and computer-integrated manufacturing, 33

O

Oregon, project in, 93

P

Partnerships: in Business Development and Training Center, 76; for computer education, 65; for economic literacy, 49-57; effective, 22-24; flexibility of, 78-79; for international trade education, 71-73; issues for, 79; position and authority of, 77-78; productive, 76-79; time and perceptions in, 76-77
Pennsylvania: educational maintenance organization in, 39-47, 93; projects in, 93, 94
Pennsylvania Innovation Network (PIN), 43
Petrides, M., 95
Pewaukee, Wisconsin, international trade program in, 67-73
PIC/Higher Education Collaboration Project, 94
Population, aging of, 6-7
Portland Community College, project at, 93
Postsecondary Adult Literacy Education Project, 95
Postsecondary Education for a Changing Economy: Resource Agent for Policies and Practices, 95
PREP, and computer-integrated manufacturing, 33

Preparing for High-Technology Careers in Computer-Integrated Manufacturing, 95
Private sector, as source of education-work integration, 13-14, 45-46
Public Broadcasting Service (PBS), 31
Public Investment in Higher Education: A Program for New England Legislators, 95

Q

Quincy, Massachusetts, worker education in, 53-54

R

Rexnord Industrial Automation Systems, and computer-integrated manufacturing, 33
Rio Salada Community College, project at, 94
Rolzinski, C. A., 2, 3, 5, 15, 75, 85, 87, 92
Rouse & Associates, and educational maintenance organization, 39, 41, 45, 46
Rural Education/Adult Development in Idaho (READI), and computer education, 59-65, 78, 81, 82, 84, 95
Rutgers University, project at, 94

S

Saint Joseph's University, corporate center MBA program of, 41-42
St. Louis Community College-Forest Park, project at, 93
Sales and Marketing Group, 44
San Diego State University, project at, 93
Sandia National Laboratories, 31
School for New Learning Graduate Program, 95
Secretaries and Administrative Assistants Advisory Group, 43
Self-employment, growth in, 8
Service Employees International Union (SEIU), and worker education, 49, 54
Service sector, growth of, 7-8
Shovers, B. A., 2, 17, 25, 77, 84-85

Siefer, N. A., 2, 17, 25, 77, 84-85
Singer, E., 12, 15
Skinner, E. F., 2, 17, 25, 77, 84-85, 93
Small business, in international trade, 67-73
Small Business Administration, 73
Society, shifts in, 6-7
Society of Manufacturing Engineers (SME), 29
Sources: of education-work integration, 13-14; issues of, 90-91
South Carolina, project in, 95
Square D, and computer-integrated manufacturing, 33
Staten Island, The College of, project at, 95
Sullivan, H., 12, 15
Summer Institute, for computer education, 63, 64
Sweden, worker planning in, 50

T

Teacher preparation: for computer education, 63; for computer-integrated manufacturing, 32
Technical Managers Group, 43
Technology: in computer-integrated manufacturing, 29-30; shifts of, 8-10; and supertech needs, 28
Technovate, and computer-integrated manufacturing, 33
TECPLAY: Technical Education and Career Planning for the Lives of Adults and Youths, 95
Tennessee, community economic development in, 83-84, 94
Thiel College, project at, 94
Toastmasters, 43
Tucker, M. S., 28, 36

U

Unions, and worker education, 49-57
United Auto Workers (UAW), and worker education, 49, 54, 56
U.S. Department of Commerce, 67-68, 73; International Trade Division of, 71, 72
U.S. Department of Education, 1
Upper Division BSN for Working RNs, 95

V

Vermont, Community Colleges of, project at, 93

W

Waukesha County Technical Institute (WCTI), International Trade Technical Center at, 67-73, 94

West Virginia Institute of Technology, project at, 95

Wisconsin: computer-integrated manufacturing in, 27-37, 95; international trade program in, 67-73, 94

Women, in labor force, 7, 8

Work. *See* Education-work integration

Worker Education for the 1980s: analysis of, 49-57, 96; background on, 49-51; conclusion on, 56-57; initiating, 51-52; lessons from, 55-56; projects of, 52-54

Workers, displaced, 8, 28

Workplace: language training in, 17-25, 93; as source of education-work integration, 13

Y

Yugoslavia, worker planning in, 50